Changing Lives with Spiritism

*Fresh Perspectives
for a New Humanity*

Heather Bollech-Fonseca

Changing Lives with Spiritism
Fresh Perspectives for a New Humanity

Published and distributed through a partnership between
Léon Denis Spiritist Group and the United States Spiritist Council

Léon Denis Spiritist Group – www.ldsg.us; www.explorespiritism.com
USSC - www.spiritist.us

Cover Design by Darcy F. Neto

Cover photography by Christine Caldwell

Editing by Daniel Fonseca, Robert Blakely, Judy Schalow, and Pamela Beaudry

ISBN: 978-0-9897835-0-7

Copyright © 2013 by Léon Denis Spiritist Group

All rights reserved. No part of this publication may be reproduced or transmitted in any form or by any means, electronic or mechanical, including photocopying, recording or any information storage and retrieval system, without the prior written permission of the copyright holder.

Printed in the United States of America

Changing Lives with Spiritism
Fresh Perspectives for a New Humanity

CONTENTS

1 A Personal Message 1
2 Why Changing Lives, Fresh Perspectives, and a New Humanity? 3
3 In Search of Truth: Have You Ever Felt This Way? 11
4 A Starting Point 19
5 Setting A Few Things Straight 27
6 What Do You Mean, "Codification"? 33
7 A Holistic View 43
8 Life and Love Are Not Lost 49
9 Spirits: Seen and Heard, but Too Seldom Mentioned 53
10 Life After Death and The Spirit World: Wow! 57
11 Reincarnation, Evolution, and Free Will 69
12 A Blessing to Forget? 77
13 Why Does God Allow Suffering? 83
14 Spiritual Mentors and Friends: The Comfort of Knowing They're There 99
15 Beware of Bad Company 105
16 Prayer 111
17 Jesus 117
18 The Spiritist Center 133
19 The Perspective From "Up Here" 141
20 The Only Way 151
Acknowledgements 167

1
A Personal Message

Dear Reader,

Perhaps you found this book in a Spiritist Center or it was lent to you by a friend. Maybe you stumbled across it in a bookstore or found it on a bench. In any case, you've somehow been led to discover Spiritism. How wonderful! If you are curious to know more about Spiritism, or if you are in search of a meaningful way to see and understand life, then this will be a great place to start.

In this book, you will not find a detailed explanation including everything there is to know about Spiritism. In fact, the scope of Spiritism is so broad and deep that one could not possibly include a complete set of specifics in a work of this kind. For those ready to delve deeper, there are many available sources. In the works published by Allan Kardec, we find the codification of Spiritist teachings. In addition, there are numerous other resources[1] – in print, online, in videos, and at Spiritist centers – where one can learn more about Spiritism and Spiritists.

Through this book, I simply wish to extend you a warm invitation to open your mind to new possibilities and perspectives, to set aside any preconceived ideas you may have about what the word Spiritism means, and to allow yourself a peek into the kinds of insights that Spiritism has to offer. If you are one of many already familiar with Spirit*ualism*, you'll also discover points that highlight details

---

[1] On the website, ExploreSpiritism.com, you will find a more comprehensive look at the teachings and practices of Spiritism, as well as recommendations for additional resources.

relevant to Spiri*tism* in particular. In any case, I ask you to consider yourself to be on the listening end of a friendly conversation through which I am able to share, in plain language infused with great enthusiasm, how valuable Spiritism is as a source of comfort, resolution, inspiration, and peace.

Though Spiritism has been around for over 150 years, I was not born into a Spiritist home or raised with knowledge of Spiritism. I come to you as someone who once had many questions and doubts concerning life, death, faith, and the meaning of it all. This began to change when some years ago I was given a copy of *The Spirits' Book*, published by Allan Kardec. From there, I embarked upon a new journey through a deeper study of Spiritism, which I found both captivating and enlightening. Over time, I was also blessed with various opportunities that made me a firm believer in Spiritist fundamentals. At the heart of Spiritism we find the existence of spirits and our ability to communicate with them, the reality of our own spiritual existence and evolution, and the powerful veracity of universal, moral truths found woven throughout various cultures and belief systems. Indeed, we are spiritual beings in the process of evolution, destined to progress and to learn about the true meaning of love.

May you discover in this book a message of hope and a new beginning. May you find relief, clarity, and the motivation to learn more about Spiritism. Finally, it is my sincere hope that through the study of Spiritism – beginning, perhaps, with this book – you may gain inner peace by leaving behind old, nagging questions and doubts, while discovering new ways to bring greater joy and fulfillment to your life.

Many blessings,

Heather Bollech-Fonseca

2
Why Changing Lives, Fresh Perspectives, and a New Humanity?

Presumably, there are people who will react to the title of this book with immediate enthusiasm. I'm guessing there will be plenty of others who will open the book out of mere curiosity or perhaps skepticism. Whatever the case, I'd like to explain why I titled the book *Changing Lives with Spiritism: Fresh Perspectives for a New Humanity.*

I think my challenge in writing this chapter was, quite frankly, where to start! After all, people come to Spiritism from all walks of life and from highly diverse backgrounds shaped by factors including education, experiences, and previously held beliefs. They also come from unique places in their lives. Their specific needs are different from those of their neighbors. Still, we are all human beings. In the end, we are not as different as we think. We all have inquiring minds, suffering souls, and the need to give and receive love. I've used that common ground as the backdrop to the text that follows.

Let's start with changing lives and fresh perspectives. I debated about which of them to mention first. In reality, these two concepts seem to go so hand in hand that I think we can discuss them together. Let's talk first about the inquiring minds. Among all of you who read this book, you inquirers know who you are. You are searching for truth because you know it's got to be out there. At times, you may want to throw your hands in the air and give up, yet a burning desire inside keeps you going. This longing is strengthened here and there by life's different experiences. Other times, you are driven by the mere churning of thoughts that race through your mind and leave your soul feeling unsettled. You've listened to many points of view, yet for one reason or another, you haven't found the source that really answers your greatest existential concerns. You want to know what this life is really about. You question why we're here, where we came from, where we're going, and why things are the way they are! The frustration can become so great that you feel somehow trapped, unable to take from existing philosophies or religions that which you consider reliable. After all, you intuitively sense that the ideal solution would be a consistently coherent and reliable source of information. Some of you are even frustrated by the fact that others believe in things you could not possibly fathom adopting as part of your own belief system. What matters most to you, however, is finding something that works for you.

Fortunately, for a countless number of individuals, Spiritism has been able to quench that thirst for truth. It presents convincing evidence regarding our spiritual existence and offers intriguing details concerning the nature of spirits. Through an evolutionary perspective on reincarnation, Spiritism brings clarity to concepts such as personal accountability, divine justice, and the nature of our Creator. By demonstrating these and many other concepts, Spiritism answers our burning questions. It fills in gaps and provides the glue that brings life's various puzzle pieces together while weeding out erroneous ideas that had previously held them apart. Time and time again, I've heard people say that as soon as they picked up *The Spirits' Book*, they were hooked. Allan Kardec, himself, wrote that upon initiating his own serious observance and study of spirit communications, he found in the phenomena answers he had searched for all his life.[2]

Aside from the inquirers, what about those who suffer? Throughout the history of our world, suffering has been ever present, and since Spiritism's inception, it has not been uncommon for suffering to be another avenue through which many have come to find consolation in its teachings. In our hours of sorrow and anguish, we inevitably become open to new ideas that may offer hope and a pathway to inner peace. People familiar with Spiritism often turn to Spiritist resources in an attempt to reach out to a friend or loved one who is in a place of pain or personal struggle. They may suggest a Spiritist book or invite that person to a Spiritist Center. Other times, it can be a loving spirit friend, in the spirit realm, who finds a way of bringing the light of Spiritism into the path of one who is walking in darkness but is ready to hear the message that can help brighten that journey.

Indeed, the new ways that Spiritist teachings help us to see life are profound enough to dry tears, strengthen wills, and inspire needed changes. Spiritism brings us the consoling certainty that life does not end at the grave, and it guarantees us a future reunion with loved ones. It affords relief to those who hear, see, or observe the action of spirits by revealing how this involves perfectly natural phenomena. Spiritism helps us to understand the reasons why we suffer and shows us specific actions that will reduce our suffering, both now and in the future. Furthermore, it explains to us that what we do not accomplish in this life, we will continue working toward achieving, both from the spirit realm, after this life, and in future material existences. Finally, it shows us that no matter

---

[2] In *Posthumous Works* (Second Part, section: "My First Initiation in Spiritism", 11th paragraph). This book is a collection of Kardec's writings that were published after his death. It is not yet translated to English.

how hard we fall, how badly we screw up, or how far we deviate from the path that leads to happiness, we will all be helped in our efforts to lift ourselves up and get back on track. Spiritism teaches how true happiness is the destiny of each and every one of us. Aside from the facts behind this enlightening education, I also like to tell people that no matter what the lesson at hand may be, the loving and compassionate way in which humanity's spiritual benefactors express these ideas to us makes their communications feel like a warm embrace from loved ones in Heaven, an embrace that tells us to cheer up, have hope, and "look here" at why everything is going to be OK. It's no wonder that Spiritism is considered, among Spiritists, to be the consoler promised by Jesus.

Finally, we all have a need for love. Notwithstanding the many religions and philosophers who have so eloquently brought us some flavor of this message, in some way, shape, or form, I can't deny that The Beatles said it perfectly with their famous song title, *All You Need Is Love*. It's true. The idea that we were made in God's image refers to the fact that we each have within us seeds of the divine source which is no less than pure and perfect love. We, in turn, have the duty to nurture and cultivate our love so that it may flourish and grow. While some are researching the brain, seeking clues as to what makes us act and perceive things in the ways that we do, the deeper answers lie in the fact that our immortal spirits do the thinking and thereby drive both the activity of the brain and the sentiments of the heart. Meanwhile, although love is one of our most basic spiritual needs, our understanding of love is still so limited. In fact, we do not truly comprehend the immensity of love that our Creator has for us, though I believe that Spiritism brings us a step closer than we've ever been before. Spiritism shows us how God's love is woven into the very fabric of the natural laws that govern all of creation. It also teaches us about evolution, which takes us through a continuity of lives and of countless different experiences. Underlying this evolutionary course is a series of progressive lessons that illuminate us on what it means to love and be loved. The Spiritist perspective on how and why we should love God, ourselves, and one another is applicable in every area of our lives. It changes how we see relationships, and it helps us to understand that love is more than something we simply *have*. Love reflects how we act and, ultimately, what we will one day become.

Why a *new humanity*? Times are changing. This is no secret. Look around, and although you will find different perspectives, you'll see that many people already realize that we are headed into a new era. Some call it ascension. Others call it an awakening. Meanwhile, certain belief systems include ideas about the coming of a final judgment or maybe even the end of the world. According to Spiritism, there is no final judgment or end of the world, as some predict, but there is a kind of awakening happening around us. This awakening reflects a transition that our planet is currently undergoing. Spiritism teaches that God's limitless creation has always been in a state of constant and progressive evolution. As part of this evolution, all worlds evolve. This includes our planet Earth. Spiritism classifies Earth as presently belonging to a category[3] called *worlds of trials and expiations*, though we are told that this planet is approaching the next category called *worlds of regeneration*.

This new world of regeneration will be reserved for spirits who have achieved, through their own efforts, a certain degree of moral evolution. This is one of many reasons behind

---

[3] See Chapter III of *The Gospel According to Spiritism* for more information regarding the categories of inhabited worlds.

the importance of developing the virtue of love. Believe it or not, Earth will one day be a much better, happier, and more harmonious place than it is today. When it reaches that point, spirits who are not willing to meet the minimum ethical standards will no longer be permitted to incarnate in such a place, that is, until they have improved their moral condition; they will accomplish the latter by living out certain experiences in worlds less evolved than the Earth. To the contrary, those spirits who *will* be allowed to come here are the ones who will represent this new humanity. The fact that we must be deserving of the right to "inherit the Earth"[4], in this new phase of regeneration, makes it imperative that we find out what standards of moral conduct and character will be required for one's incarnation into this more advanced world. Moreover, it illustrates why we must take a good look at ourselves to assess what improvements we should be making in our own thoughts and behaviors. For these reasons, the teachings of Spiritism are such an important asset to humanity, and they need to be shared. This reminds me of a statement from the spirit of Dr. Bezerra de Menezes[5], which I would like to share with you in a fitting conclusion to this

---

[4] The New Testament, Matthew 5:5: "Blessed are the meek, for they will inherit the earth."

[5] Adolfo Bezerra de Menezes (1831-1900) was a man of strong intelligence, sound moral character, sincere humility, and a great heart. Once a respected politician, he eventually left his political career to become a doctor. As a doctor, he earned the nickname "doctor of the poor" for his dedication to serving those most in need and helping the afflicted by any means he could. After receiving a translation of *The Spirits' Book*, Dr. Bezerra, as he is commonly referred to, also became an avid student of Spiritism. He then went on to assume a prominent role in the Brazilian Spiritist movement, laboring in the dissemination of Spiritism's consoling teachings and working diligently to promote unification among the diverse groups of Spiritist workers and proponents. Since his disincarnation in 1900, Dr. Bezerra has become a beloved spiritual benefactor. From the spiritual realm, he has remained committed to the cause of supporting the Spiritist movement and promoting moral progress among men and women on Earth.

chapter. In a message[6] psychographed by the medium Francisco Cândido Xavier, Dr. Bezerra wrote these inspiring words:

"Let us, therefore, be courageous in disseminating the Spiritist doctrine which rescues the Gospel from a literal interpretation, making it an instrument in the formation of a new humanity; let us radiate the divine Master's inspiration and influence, through our emotions and ideas, through our rules of conduct and behavior, and through our words and examples...".

With these words, Dr. Bezerra points the way to a new humanity. Fresh perspectives such as those found in Spiritism will inevitably change lives. Love and compassion, stemming from a renewed understanding of both our existence and of one another, will be the standard way of life on this precious planet that so many will yet come to call *home*.

---

[6] From the message "Problems of the World" by spirit author Dr. Bezerra de Menezes, in the book "O Espírito da Verdade" [Title translation: "The Spirit of Truth"; to date, an English translation of the book has not been published.], psychographed by the mediums Francisco Cândido Xavier and Waldo Viera, published by The Brazilian Spiritist Federation (FEB), © 1961 by FEB.

3
In Search of Truth: Have You Ever Felt This Way?

Personally, I came to Spiritism with a lot of questions and doubts. Fortunately, I was raised in a very loving, faith-based home. However, at some point during my adolescence, I started to feel an increasing sense of confusion when it came to topics typically associated with religion, philosophy, and matters concerning our very existence. I wanted to have the kind of faith in God that I saw in other people, regardless of their religious affiliations, but I had many questions for which I did not find answers that fit, at least for me. That was until I found Spiritism. Jump ahead to the years I have since lived as a Spiritist. During this time, many individuals have told me that they, too, had struggled with similar doubts but also felt a sense of resolution upon encountering the reasoning elaborated throughout Spiritist teachings, books, and other resources. With this experience in mind, I'm confident that there are plenty of people who feel frustrated, as I once did. If you can at all relate, then this chapter is for you. In general, I ask all readers to bear with me, since I'm writing here about my personal experience, but I think you will agree that any body of knowledge capable of answering these types of questions is at least worth learning more about.

Some of the doubts I once had were specifically theological, whereas others were more generalized. I believe I would have gone through this soul-searching experience, regardless of any particular faith, or lack thereof, in which I could have been raised. However, given my background, my theological questions pertained more to concepts that generally fall within the scope of some popular Christian teachings. I'm not intentionally excluding other perspectives;

this is just my own experience. While sharing these personal reflections, I will refrain from mentioning every religious point that I had my qualms about. In fairness, some ideas really deserve an in-depth discussion that is beyond the scope of this book.

I cannot recall exactly when I started to question certain aspects of what I had been exposed to, in religious settings. I do remember, however, coming home from school, after learning about things like dinosaurs, fossils, and other geographic records, recognizing a need to reconcile all that with what I'd been taught regarding creation. This always bothered me a bit, but I think the frustration culminated in a high school biology class assignment in which, after learning about evolution and watching a video of a debate between one person with a creationist view and another with an evolutionist view, we were required to write an essay in which we basically had to pick sides. The assignment forced us to explain whether we believed in creation or evolution, and why, thus insinuating that the two were necessarily mutually exclusive!

I recall fretting over that essay and how to answer. I believed the evidence made the case for evolution. However, I also felt that no matter how far back in time one could, either definitively or theoretically, trace the formation of the world around us, the basic, most fundamental building blocks had to come from somewhere. I also felt that there was so much order and beauty in nature, from the microscopic to the macroscopic, that it was hard to believe it was all nothing but random chance. For these reasons, in the end, I eventually chose to make my argument for creation, at least for the purposes of that assignment. My real convictions went unresolved. Finally, one day, further down the road, I felt great relief upon reading the fourth question in *The Spirits'*

Book, which asks, "Where may we find proof for the existence of God?", and the answer, "In the axiom that you apply to all your sciences: 'There is no effect without a cause.'". This is followed by Kardec's comment that "to believe in God, we need only to behold the works of creation."[7] I found these statements reassuring, as they confirmed what I had believed must be true.

In spite of those who take the literal view, I know there are many who have long seen the descriptions of creation as being symbolic, regardless of a particular religion, and I know of the concept of intelligent design. However, what I appreciated in Spiritism was not only the philosophical elements that make similar arguments, but the details found in Spiritism to support them[8]. Through Spiritism, we gain clarity as to why creation (formation by some kind of intelligent Creator) and evolution are not opposing concepts. We do not have to pin God, in one corner, against science in the other!

I believe it was about the same time as the experience noted above that I started to be quite bothered by one particular question. I saw the different religions of the world and contemplated their tendency to be, to greater or lesser degrees, geographically concentrated, even if there were several such concentrations around the globe. Keep in mind that this was before the days of the internet, which has

---

[7] See question and answer #4 in *The Spirits' Book* by Allan Kardec [original title in French: *Le Livre des Espirits*, published in 1857 with 2nd edition in 1860], translation © 2006 by the International Spiritist Council, authorized edition printed in 2010 by Edicei of America.

[8] This includes Allan Kardec's chapters concerning the origin and transformation of the Earth in his book *Genesis*; text from the spirit Emmanuel, regarding the planetary genesis and the history of civilization, in the book *On the Way to the Light;* and basic fundamentals of Spiritism which include details that we might otherwise perceive only intuitively or through a certain degree of personal reasoning.

revolutionized global communication and information sharing. At the same time, I saw that the proponents, teachers, and believers of each different religion felt that their own belief systems were essentially right, by default making the others wrong in any given points of discrepancy. Meanwhile, there are millions of individuals who live out their entire lives practicing the faith of their families or cultures with no thought about other religions. Even more significant are those who have no access and/or exposure to other teachings or beliefs. I couldn't help but wonder, considering that we only have one life to live (or so I thought), how a loving God would allow souls to be born into circumstances in which they'd naturally believe in fallacies, especially without even hearing about that which is true! This is especially noteworthy when you consider such key matters as origin, destiny, salvation, and the meaning of life and death. This very unsettling worry was not removed from my mind until I encountered Spiritism.

Perhaps spawned by this question of how there could be births into opposing belief systems, with no opportunity to learn of the "right" path, or maybe just as a natural consequence of following a separate thought process, I also wanted to know why there was so much disparity in the world. I questioned why God would have us live in such extremes, especially considering that some lives entailed very pleasant experiences while others were sources of great pain. Why, I wondered, are some born into wealth with all the material comforts while others have to live in places of extreme poverty, starvation, and the like? Why are some raised in loving homes, safe communities, or relatively stable countries while others grow up in emotionally or physically harmful home settings with danger all around them or with the persistent presence of violence and war? Why do some have opportunities for education while others live in communities that cannot even afford basic school supplies or don't believe in educating certain classes or genders? Why do some have healthy and well-functioning bodies throughout their whole lives while some children are born with physical challenges, including ones that are even painful for others to see?

That list of inquiries could go on and on, but you get the idea. I know we hear that God has his reasons, even if we do not understand them, or that through these experiences, we can learn powerful lessons. Still, I wondered where the fairness was, if some had easy lessons and others had such hard ones. In any case, did God create us differently? If so, where were the criteria for that? Where was the justice in it?

To my relief, Kardec included a particular chapter in *The Spirits' Book* in which he presents questions of this very nature, along with his own commentary. Interestingly, Kardec asks about other disparities as well. He questions our differences related to personalities, abilities, affinities, and character. Examples of this type could include the following: Why do some people, even from the time they are very young, have a calm and easy going nature, coupled with a natural inclination to be kind and compassionate, while others are immediately restless and agitated or at some point reveal a tendency to be unsympathetic, disrespectful, and sometimes even cruel? Why do some individuals have an amazingly superior intelligence or other natural talent while others struggle to cope with learning disabilities? Why do certain people have such strong interests in one area while others discover a deep passion for some other subject? Such diffcrences are even more interesting when they are found in twins, or even siblings close in age, raised by the same parents in nearly the same setting (thus diminishing the nature vs. nurture question). Again, the list could go on.

In his commentary on these disparities, Kardec points out that a mere contemplation of such inequalities could provide significant *philosophical* evidence for the existence of reincarnation. The philosophical argument for reincarnation, however, is also strongly supported by the answers and teachings derived from spirit communications. Throughout various Spiritist resources, we find numerous illustrations of how reincarnation provides the missing puzzle piece to answer those questions about our otherwise inexplicable differences. As Kardec writes, "If we, as so many others, have adopted the doctrine of the plurality of existences, it is not only because it has come from the Spirits, but because it has seemed to us to be the most logical and the only one that resolves issues that until now have been unresolvable."[9]

There is one theological matter that I would like to address in this chapter, and that is the idea of eternal punishment, another concept that always bothered me. Again, there are many people who see the idea of hell as symbolic, but there are many others who believe in the literal interpretation and trust that eternal chastisement does exist. Yet how could this be so? How could we believe that a perfectly just and loving God, who wants us to learn about and exercise the virtue of forgiveness, would send his own children to suffer for all of eternity for their wrongdoing if we only have one lifetime to get things right? This principle teaches that whether people buckle under the struggles of life or fall victim to the horrible ideas in their own minds, they will never, ever, have the opportunity to redeem themselves

---

[9] Ch V "Considerations Concerning the Plurality of Existences" in Part II of *The Spirits' Book* by Allan Kardec [original title in French: *Le Livre des Espirits*, published in 1857 with 2nd edition in 1860], translation © 2006 by the International Spiritist Council, authorized edition printed in 2010 by Edicei of America.

from the lamentable choices they made, no matter how deeply they regret their actions.

Granted, there are belief systems that teach their views on what we can do now to obtain eternal happiness and suffer no further consequences for our immoral actions. However, do we really think it's fair that a person who lived a highly noble and morally upright life could experience the same afterlife conditions as one who consistently acted with no apparent regard for others? The first would have spread love and happiness wherever he or she went, demonstrating an innate sense of kindness, compassion, and concern for others. The second would likely have acted in inappropriate, cruel, selfish, sometimes even abhorrent ways. Do we believe that there are no consequences for misdeeds and no rewards for virtuous behavior?

Suppose we set aside these types of questions. What about those who don't adhere to the prescribed requirements for eternal happiness before this life is over? Again, we are back to the God who has somehow a limited degree of forgiveness. Furthermore, let's understand that people are born in different places around the globe where they might never receive these teachings that advise the *right* way to ensure one's "ticket to salvation". Why would they deserve anything less than, at minimum, the same chances given to anyone else? As if these questions were not enough, we should also stop and ask ourselves this: if we are so fortunate as to deserve everlasting peace and joy, how can we truly be happy in the afterlife knowing that others, from strangers to perhaps some particular loved ones, may not be so fortunate and could instead suffer eternally?

Fortunately, we now have the means to put all these doubts to rest. For one thing, Spiritism demonstrates that eternal punishment does not exist[10]. It is time that we forget about this tormenting view of the future. The truth is that in accordance with our own effort and merit, we are all destined to attain true happiness. Likewise, when it comes to those questions concerning the origin of life, Spiritism is able to provide logical explanations that acknowledge both the spiritual and material elements rather than making them mutually exclusive. Finally, we no longer have to grapple with those disconcerting observations that, in the absence of rational explanations, leave us questioning the justice behind disparities we see in nearly every aspect of life. In the principles of Spiritist teachings, we find the clues to unlock a new vision of divine justice. In this book, you will read about some of those principles, including free will, accountability, action and reaction, conscience, reparation, renewal, and spiritual evolution. Upon leaving behind old, mistaken notions, so as to look at life from the perspective illuminated by these concepts, humanity will truly find meaningful and inspiring faith and will, thereby, make great strides in its march toward progress.

---

[10] Suggested reading: Kardec's *The Spirits' Book*: Part 4, Chapter II "Future Joys and Sorrows"; Kardec's *Heaven and Hell*: Part One – Chapter IV "Hell", Chapter V "Purgatory", Chapter VI "The Doctrine of Eternal Punishment", and Chapter VII "Future Punishment According to Spiritism"; Kardec's *What is Spiritism*: 12th, 13th, and 14th questions of section "Third Dialogue – The Priest" found in Chapter I.

4
A Starting Point

For those who are new to Spiritism, we will need a starting point for discussion. Before I narrow in or elaborate on any particular aspect of Spiritism, I believe you should have a general idea of the bigger picture. No matter how deeply one delves into the many aspects and applications of Spiritist thought, the bottom line will always come back to the same fundamental building blocks I'd like to present. The following is a very brief outline of some of the basic principles of Spiritist teachings.

To begin, Spiritists do believe there is something greater than all else that exists, and we call this God. In a way, it may seem as though we personify God, for you will hear us make reference, for example, to what God wants for us, how God is loving, or that God is our Father and we are his children. I see these as ways we have, within our presently limited knowledge and vocabulary, to express and understand the attributes and action of this something that is all-powerful and is the Creator of everything in existence. After all, the first question in Allan Kardec's work, *The Spirits' Book*, very wisely asks not "Who is God?", but "What is God?", and the answer is that God is "the Supreme Intelligence, the First Cause of all things." This same first chapter also attributes these descriptions to God: *eternal, immutable, immaterial, singular, all-powerful,* and *supremely just and good*, and yet we are told that such depictions provide a complete picture only from our human point of view. This is because there are things our language still cannot define. Someday, we will have new ways to comprehend and articulate ideas about our Creator. In the meantime, to fully comprehend the true meaning of that definition and those six attributes listed, we certainly have much learning to keep us busy.

As Spiritists, we believe in life after death and the immortality of our souls. We typically refer to our immortal souls as spirits. Through Spiritism, we study the origin, nature, and destiny of spirits. In other words, we learn about where we come from, what we are doing here, and where we are going when this material lifetime ends. As you may or may not be aware, we also believe that this life we are living is not our first, nor our last; we believe in reincarnation, or the rebirth of souls into new bodies. Perhaps you already have some ideas about reincarnation, whether they are based on a certain religion, a personal experience, or the findings of a particular study. In this book, you will learn more about the *Spiritist* understanding of reincarnation.

Another concept that people quite readily associate with Spiritism is communication with those no longer living on Earth. It is true that we do believe in such communications. However, we are not the first, nor the only people to do so, as this practice is actually found throughout history. Therefore, there are a great number of misconceptions among the general public regarding the way these communications are defined, understood, and carried out, with regard to Spiritist beliefs and practices. I will provide some clarifications on this later in the book. In addition, you can always learn more through an in-depth study of Spiritism. In general, the ability to perceive or communicate with such spirits can take many forms, including the capacity to see them, hear them, or receive communication from them in one way or another. We refer to this faculty as mediumship. Those who have one or more developed forms of the faculty are called mediums. As you will read more about later, the

Spiritist philosophy was actually derived from communications with spirits.

◊ ◊ ◊

According to Spiritism, evolution is constant. God is continuously creating, and everything created evolves, which means that it transforms over time. In this case, we say that such transformations bring about progress, meaning growth and development. We learn that even our worlds, including planets, actually evolve, as do the beings that inhabit them. Yes, we also believe that in this vast, truly limitless creation, planet Earth is not the only home to living beings. In Spiritism, this was first introduced in Allan Kardec's *The Spirits' Book*. In *The Gospel According to Spiritism*, Kardec expanded on the idea in a chapter entitled, "There are Many Dwellings in My Father's House", which he opened with reference to that very statement from Jesus[11].

Spiritism teaches that as human spirits, we are evolving, or progressing, both morally and intellectually. Given that we are created at different times and that we each evolve at our own pace[12], we can find human spirits throughout creation at all different stages of moral and intellectual evolution. In turn, these worlds that we inhabit also exist at varying stages of evolution. By this design, they provide the conditions appropriate to our developmental needs as we progress through different levels of advancement.

Evolution is the process by which our spirits transform. We began in a state of simplicity and unawareness, acting largely based on instinct. Our destiny is a point at

---

[11] The New Testament: John 14: 1–3.
[12] You will read more about this later.

which we will have acquired complete intellectual knowledge and moral virtue. This is referred to as complete purification, or relative perfection. As it is not possible to complete this evolutionary process in just one lifetime, we are given several lifetimes. Through them, we are able to transform gradually. In reality, we live one continuous life as immortal spirits, and these lifetimes that I refer to represent our numerous incarnations in material worlds, where we assume different personalities and encounter a great variety of living conditions. These incarnations aid in our spiritual progress by affording us an immensely wide spectrum of interconnected experiences.

The nature, function, and evolution of worlds and living beings are all regulated by what we refer to as a set of divine or natural laws. Through developments in science and intellectual progress, we have already discovered many of the laws that govern matter; others are still unknown. Meanwhile, there is also a set of moral laws that govern the processes and principles of evolution. They are studied in detail throughout Spiritism. To give you an idea, they include the individual laws of worship, labor, reproduction, preservation, destruction, society, progress, equality, and freedom, plus the great law of justice, love and charity. These laws determine the various aspects of our spiritual existence and the course of our moral development. As we evolve, we acquire greater knowledge of these laws. In part, we gain such awareness through study. To a large extent, we also learn through experience by exercising our free will. Free will is always granted in accordance with our stage of progress and comes with an equal degree of accountability for our actions.

The ultimate function of the moral laws is to guide us on a pathway of knowledge and love. The ethical development that we undergo takes us through many lessons and a multitude of lifetimes as we learn how to understand and embody the true meaning of love. Meanwhile, as appropriate to our present spiritual state on Earth, there are many sources of moral teachings available to all who seek them. As Spiritists, we appreciate any resources that will help us to become better, kinder, and more compassionate, to have more faith, and to discover a deeper sense of meaning, purpose, and joy in life. Our primary point of reference, in this sense, is Jesus' moral lessons, which we find clarified and illuminated by Spiritist teachings.

◊ ◊ ◊

Now, how are we doing so far? If you're still with me, I'd like to include a few more concepts to build on. If you are concerned, don't worry. You can follow the rest of the book with what I've outlined to this point. However, for those interested, I think it's worth it to provide more supporting details regarding some of the ideas that will later be mentioned or discussed.

First of all, Spiritism teaches that within God's creation, there are two basic elements – matter and spirit. Bear with me as I add some details to that statement; later, you will see how things start to come together. Matter, one of the basic, universal elements, exists in a great, perhaps limitless, variety of modified forms. On one end of the spectrum are the most ethereal forms, meaning those least ponderable, or least tangible. They are closest to matter's most primitive state. At the other extreme are the forms of a highly ponderable and most dense condition. This is where we find matter as we typically know it on Earth, meaning that we can see it, touch it, feel it, hear the sounds it makes, etc. For the sake of illustration, let's take H_2O and just visualize, for a moment, that it represents the most basic form of matter[13]. A highly dense and ponderable form of this substance would be frozen water. However, it can also exist as a liquid or in a gaseous state, meaning evaporated to some degree. Once evaporated, it can still be concentrated enough such that we are able to see it, or it can be so far evaporated that we cannot see it or feel it, even if it is present right before us, or around us. The evaporation of water to the point where we cannot detect it is, in a way, like the etherealized form of matter. Of course, this is only an analogy, but it helps to make these concepts a little more digestible[14].

While one general element of the universe includes everything that is in some way material, the other is completely immaterial. It is what we call spirit, or the intelligent principle of the universe. Most of the time, however, when we use the term, spirit, we are referring to individual spirits as I did earlier in this chapter. When we talk about these individual, living spirits, we refer to an individualized form of the intelligent principle. In human spirits, we say that this intelligent principle permanently retains its individuality. This means that once we as human spirits are created, we remain the same singular being from that point forward. Over the course of time, we develop in knowledge and awareness, whereby we always build on previous levels and degrees of progress.

Finally, having introduced matter and spirit, we can now talk about the material world and the spiritual world. I wanted to offer a few details that may help those having a bit

---

[13] In Spiritism, this most basic form of matter is referred to as the "universal cosmic fluid." For further details on the universal cosmic fluid and its derivatives in the ethereal state (called "fluids"), see Kardec's book *Genesis*, Section I of Chapter XIV in Part II.

[14] For further details on spirit and matter as universal elements, see Chapter II of Kardec's *The Spirits' Book*.

of trouble conceptualizing these two different worlds. Previously, I mentioned that our many lives offer us the opportunity to experience a great variety of diverse living conditions. Now let me explain that these living conditions are experienced in two different dimensions. This is not so different from the already familiar reference points of Heaven and Earth. However, through Spiritist teachings, we have new information that gives us a more detailed and somewhat different understanding of those familiar concepts.

These two dimensions are what we call the material and spiritual realms (a.k.a. worlds, dimensions, or planes), and they co-exist alongside one another. The *material* realm is made up of matter in a more ponderable form, and the spirits that inhabit the material world are in what we call the *incarnate* state, meaning that they are "in the flesh". This is the condition you and I are in at this moment. We have a soul, a temporary, physical body made of flesh, and a second body made of a less ponderable form of matter. We call this second body the *perispirit*. The perispirit remains with the soul, throughout its incarnations and in between them. One of its functions is to allow the thinking, immaterial soul to act upon the purely material body.

In contrast to the material realm, the *spiritual* realm is made up of matter in a more ethereal state, and the spirits who inhabit the spiritual world are in what we call the *discarnate* state[15]. They only have their soul and their perispirit[16]. When the life of our own temporary, physical bodies comes to an end, we will disconnect from those material garments and return to inhabit the spiritual realm. Down the road, we will eventually come back again to begin a

---

[15] This is sometimes called the *errant* state.

[16] This perispirit is the physical form that people actually perceive when they are able to see discarnate spirits.

new, temporary existence in the material world. The repetition of this cycle is what we call reincarnation.

◊ ◊ ◊

There you have it. God, spirits, and evolution in two worlds: these are the fundamental building blocks of Spiritist philosophy, as revealed through the observation, study, and practice of Spiritist science. It is through the concepts that I've outlined in this chapter that we can begin to form a new and more meaningful idea of life itself. In the next few chapters, you will encounter further clarifications that address common misconceptions concerning the term *Spiritism*. You will also find an overview of the principal literary works that form the foundation of Spiritist teachings and studies, otherwise known as the books of the Spiritist codification.

5
Setting A Few Things Straight

Newcomers to Spiritism, meaning Spiritism as codified by Allan Kardec, often experience a first phase of learning that involves the dispelling of old notions. These previously held beliefs are frequently philosophical, spiritual, or theological in nature. In discovering the clarity, logic, and detail found in Spiritism, new students begin to see life, or certain aspects of it, from a fresh angle. Other times, they find out that Spiritism is not what they envisioned, and they are surprised to learn about the true activities of Spiritists. This book addresses what Spiritism is and what it brings to humanity. However, I would like to say a few words about what Spiritism is *not*, and these ideas will be further clarified throughout subsequent chapters.

There are people who feel almost immediately taken aback when they first hear or read the term Spiritism. They begin to associate it with a number of different things, and depending on how they hear about it, they may link it with certain negative connotations. This reflects both a lack of awareness, as well as the lack of habit (in our culture) of talking about spirits in any sort of natural way, especially not with the development of ideas and vision found in Spiritism. This kind of reaction is not surprising considering the myriad of different beliefs and practices that have been classified as "Spiritism" ever since Allan Kardec first coined the term in the 1800s. Please be clear that when I use the terms *Spiritism* or *Spiritist*, I am always referring to that which is in line with the codification of the spirits' teachings as established by the works of Allan Kardec.

Later, you will read an introductory description regarding the use of mediumship by Spiritists in Spiritist Centers. Mediumship is a naturally occurring human faculty[17], by which incarnate beings can communicate with discarnate ones. Contrary to what the uninformed may assume, Spiritists do not use mediumship for entertainment or other frivolous purposes, nor to cast spells or do anything else, for that matter, with the intention of causing harm to anyone. We also do not practice fortune telling, horoscope reading, or ask the spirits to make any predictions about the future. All the above are activities that elevated spirits, both in terms of knowledge and moral character, would never participate in. We only use mediumship for the purpose of learning, receiving guidance and consolation, and helping to improve the condition of others, both incarnate and discarnate.

By the same token, we do not perform or believe in exorcisms, nor do we utilize any other means to *force* an ignorant or ill-willed spirit to cease its disturbing influence on an incarnate individual. Instead, Spiritism clarifies that true, moral superiority is the type of authority recognized and considered among spirits. In cases of spiritual disturbance, where mediumship is used to provide assistance, this is done with compassion for both the incarnate and discarnate involved. The discarnate spirit is not forced, but counseled, and the incarnate individual is educated about how to avoid such influences.

---

[17] As noted in a later chapter, we all experience some degree of influence from spirits, such as the suggestion of thoughts received by intuition. However, not everyone presently registers the spirits' influence with the degree of sensitivity found in those having an ostensive, or expressive, form of the mediumistic faculty. It is by this ostensive form that we typically classify someone as a "medium". Through the work of these mediums, we communicate with the spirit realm.

In Spiritism, we don't use Ouija boards, tarot cards, incense, candles, charms, or the like, as we have no need for them, nor do we have much faith in their utility. We understand how to communicate with spirits and benefit from our natural relationship with the spirit world in a much more effective way. Finally, while many are quick to issue warnings about what they call "dangers of the occult", we learn, from resources like Kardec's *The Mediums' Book* and others, how to distinguish the varying nature of spirits according to their language, knowledge, and behavior. We also learn how to engage in mediumship safely, aided by the protection of noble spirits who collaborate with us in effort to bring light and love where it is needed.

Another important thing to know about Spiritism and Spiritists is that their work is done in the absence of financial compensation. This means, for example, that those who benefit from mediumship-based forms of assistance at a Spiritist Center will not be asked to pay for this help. Likewise, Spiritist groups offer additional forms of social and community service, again without charging those assisted. In addition, there are generally no paid positions within the ranks of workers at a Spiritist Center. This includes all roles involved in the management of the Center, as well as the public speakers. Most typically, it will also include the many individuals who perform tasks needed to maintain the facility and assure that the meetings and other services run smoothly. This is all done voluntarily[18] and, quite commonly, by individuals whose weekly schedules include outside forms of

---

[18] In some cases, there may be individuals who are paid for labor involved with work including book publishing, janitorial maintenance, cooking, babysitting, transportation, etc. However, this is not in most Centers and if found, it is more likely to be in those locations that have become large facilities. It will not include work done by speakers and other instructors, the Center's administrators, mediums, pass-givers, etc.

employment. As a related comment, Spiritism teaches that we all have a direct relationship with God, one that is as strong as our own faith and the integrity of our thoughts and actions. In the Spiritist Center there are no individuals who are specially ordained. Those in a position to teach about Spiritism are simply individuals who have done a great deal of studying and have the knowledge, desire, and ability to share it with others.

Aside from the above remarks concerning activities of Spiritists, there are a couple of philosophical clarifications I would like to make regarding Spiritism. First, knowing that Spiritism involves the belief in reincarnation, it is common for newcomers to wonder if this works like a perpetually spinning wheel. They also wonder if we can ever reincarnate as animals. To facilitate a better absorption of the ideas I will present in later chapters, I think it is best we clear this up. Spiritism does not teach about reincarnation in this way. The Spiritist understanding of reincarnation is that of a progressive, evolutionary process, one that is forward marching. Due to some unfortunate choices in their exercise of free will, spirits can and often do stagnate, or they may reveal that they are not as advanced as once believed. However, they never regress in development. Likewise, in certain severe cases misbehaving human spirits may be forced to incarnate in less advanced worlds, but they will not reincarnate in the body of less evolved life forms, such as animals.

A second philosophical clarification has to do with the topic of suffering. In Spiritist literature and other resources, you will find explanations of how suffering always has a purpose, according to the workings of natural law. In one way or another, it always serves to aid in our spiritual progress. I will talk more about this later, in a chapter dedicated to this subject. However, given Spiritist teachings about the value of suffering and the educational, corrective, and curative roles of our various trials and tribulations, there is a common misconception that Spiritists actually look for suffering in order to obtain its stated benefits. This, however, is categorically untrue. The fact is that Spiritism does not teach us to *seek* suffering, but rather how to understand, endure, overcome, and avoid it.

The final misunderstanding that I would like to address is, ironically, almost the opposite of what I just mentioned. I have heard general criticism about what some see as the emergence of new-age, "feel good" philosophies and belief systems. Perhaps some uninformed individuals will classify Spiritism in this way. What I would like to make clear is that the Spiritist message does not come sugar-coated in any way. To be certain, Spiritism brings a positive message. For example, it presents clear reason to believe that everyone is destined to attain true happiness, that God does not punish, and that even though we must accept the consequences of our actions, we should make every effort to forgive ourselves for our mistakes. It shows us that our behaviors are more important than any particular philosophical or religious beliefs. It also clarifies the existence of spirits and even demonstrates that there are good and noble spirits with whom one can communicate. Furthermore, Spiritist teachings do not instill fear. Instead, they inspire courage, hope, and compassion. They teach us about ways to seek happiness in this world, and they allow us to envision the future with optimistic faith, rather than doubt, confusion, or apprehension.

Indeed, Spiritism offers many uplifting teachings. Alongside them, however, the Spiritist philosophy does involve some pretty harsh realities, such as the painful consequences triggered by our misuse of free will and by the choices that take us far from the pathway of love. While we talk about the wonders of progressive and happy places in the spiritual realm, we also learn about the darkness, shadows, and suffering found in the lower regions of the spirit world. The latter are inhabited by spirits whose negative vibrations draw them to such an environment. Though we believe in good and loving spirits, we are also well aware of the less evolved ones whose intentions are not always kind or innocent. They may even be ill-willed or seek to cause harm. The point is that knowledge is power. Fortunately, Spiritism makes us aware of these issues while illustrating them in a balanced way, presenting both sides of the bigger picture. From the Spiritist perspective, the inspirational truth inevitably shines through the darkness, brightening our vision with understanding, hope, and a renewed and powerful faith.

6
What Do You Mean, "Codification"?

When we talk about the five fundamental Spiritist books all published by Allan Kardec, we refer to this collection as the *codification of Spiritism*. *Codification* is a word that is not often used in popular language. Therefore, people who hear or read this sometimes jump to hasty, misinformed assumptions about Spiritism. However, *codification* simply refers to the act of arranging something in a systematic order, collecting the principles of a system of law into one body. This is exactly what Kardec did with all the clarifications, explanations, and revelations concerning natural law, which he deduced or derived from his study of spirit communications. Kardec observed, studied, compared, tested, organized, and compiled all of this information into the body of knowledge he ultimately came to refer to as Spiritism. Without going into great depth, I would like to provide an overview of Kardec and each of these books.

Allan Kardec and the important work he completed have yet to be discovered by most of humanity, yet this was truly a very special person with an important role to fulfill. The course and direction of his life, as well as his own personal characteristics prepared him for the work he would one day complete. Without failure, he valiantly answered the calling and completed this divine undertaking, to the benefit of individuals around the world and for generations to come. When you have an opportunity to read more about the history of Spiritism[19], you will also learn more about Allan Kardec,

---

[19] For a discussion on the developments that comprise the history of Spiritism, as well as details about Allan Kardec's life, his initial exposure to the popular spiritualist phenomena of the mid 19th century, and his

himself. You will then discover why the details of his life, his character, and the way he approached his study of both the spirits and their communications all lend a serious credibility to the body of knowledge that he assembled. Allan Kardec is actually the pen name of the Frenchman, Hippolyte Leon Denizard Rivail (1804–1869), who used this pseudonym to publish his Spiritist works. In the Spiritist setting, he is almost always referred to as Allan Kardec, which is also the case with every other chapter in this book.

Prior to his encounter with and study of spirits, Rivail was already an established man of great intellect. Highly knowledgeable in many subjects and fluent in multiple languages, this disciple and collaborator of the renowned educational reformer, Johann Heinrich Pestalozzi, was not only a great scholar but also a very important and influential educator of his time. Rivail's sharp mind and ability to facilitate learning in others were of great importance to his role as the codifier of Spiritism. So, too, were his healthy degree of skepticism and his tremendous capacity for logic, reasoning, critical thinking, and judgment, the latter of which becomes refreshingly apparent to those who study his works. Rivail's persistence and determination, proven more than once prior to his investigation of the spirits, served to sustain him in light of all the opposition he would later face. These qualities also gave him the strength to make many personal sacrifices as he diligently labored in the dissemination of their teachings. Finally, the strength of his moral character, indispensable to someone charged with the task to which he was called, was evidenced by the degree of effort that Rivail, or Kardec, made in order to share the spirits' teachings for the benefit of all humanity, as well as in his ability to elaborate on

---

subsequent study of spirit communications, please see the History section of the ExploreSpiritism.com website.

the spirits' statements with very helpful, supporting explanations and illustrations.

The Spirits' Book was the first book Kardec published, as a result of his studies of the spirits. The first edition was published in 1857. This fascinating work contains a series of 1,019 questions and answers concerning the immortality of the soul. These answers were obtained through communications with spirits, including communications received by mediums that Kardec personally worked with, as well as the multitude of communications obtained by other mediums and subsequently provided to him.[20] In reviewing, dissecting, analyzing, and comparing the information coming from these multiple sources, Kardec took nothing for granted. He carefully looked for trustworthy and useful information. He recognized that the degree of reliability in the different spirits' answers and statements was just as varied as the spirits' own levels of spiritual advancement, and he proceeded accordingly with cautious judgment and proper discernment. Ultimately, the questions and answers were carefully assembled in such a way that makes this book a captivating and enlightening read.

In general, Spiritism addresses the origin, nature, and destiny of spirits. *The Spirits' Book* outlines the basic principles of Spiritist teachings. It also delves into a great number of very specific and interesting topics; this becomes readily apparent to anyone who just glances at the table of contents. Through the insights found in *The Spirits' Book*, life takes on great meaning. We understand where we come from, why we are here (on Earth), what happens when this lifetime ends, and where we are going after that. The spirits' answers and Kardec's complementary remarks explain concepts with

---

[20] These mediums were not only from France but also from places around the world.

impressive logic and reason. Furthermore, they restore faith in a greater power that embodies perfect wisdom and justice. Time and time again, newcomers encountering this book breathe a sigh of relief as the unfolding chapters begin to provide resolution to their long held questions and doubts.

In 1861, Kardec published ***The Mediums' Book***. The scope of this book, both unique and comprehensive, makes it different from other books one typically finds concerning the subject of mediumship. For example, it has an entire section that explains the many types of mediumship and how they work. It also includes some discussion on the development of mediumship. However, it does not serve as a "how-to" guide giving the impression that anyone can attain a fully developed ability to see, hear, channel, or otherwise communicate with the spirit realm. From the start, Kardec makes it clear that his book is not a training guide intended to prepare anyone to serve as an intermediary between the spiritual and material realms. We all experience some degree of influence from spirits, such as the suggestion of thoughts received by intuition. However, not everyone registers the spirits' influence with the degree of sensitivity found in those having an ostensive, or expressive, form of the mediumistic faculty. We typically classify the latter as *mediums*.

Another important distinction to point out is that Kardec's book does not exemplify or encourage professional mediumship. Instead, it emphasizes the role of mediumship as a means of dutifully serving God and our fellow beings both incarnate and discarnate. It highlights mediumship as a gift through which the medium is a vehicle or channel for the spirits' ideas, not the owner of them, and it makes the point that the absence of financial gain not only lends credibility to a self-proclaimed medium, but also helps to keep a medium's objectives properly focused on benefitting others.

Unlike the majority of other individuals, mediums have an ostensive form of this faculty and are, therefore, able to communicate with spirits. Contrary to what one might deduce from that fact, mediums are not to be seen as privileged or morally advanced. This is another clarification found in *The Mediums' Book*[21], where we learn that the mediumistic faculty is neutral and that its use will reveal the moral character of the medium. We also learn that individuals from all different levels are endowed with mediumship, even those who may have the tendency to use it for malevolent purposes. The faculty is granted as an opportunity for them to better themselves by using it in benefit of others. It is by their own free will that they take advantage of such a gift or not.

Unfortunately, the actions of deceitful individuals – pretending to be mediums in communication with the spirit world but, in one way or another, revealing themselves to be impostors – have, no doubt, aggravated public skepticism about the existence of this faculty. Indeed, there was much doubt about mediumship in Kardec's time, just as there is today. In the first section of this book, Kardec addresses those concerns with a discussion of the mere existence of spirits and mediums. Later, by demonstrating the serious character of Spiritism, he dispels notions of frivolity and charlatanism within the Spiritist practice of mediumship.

In *The Mediums' Book*, Kardec also addresses those who oppose mediumship for fear of danger. He explains that it is a natural phenomenon, one that undeniably exists whether we seek it or not. He also clarifies why it is better to understand how mediumship functions – precisely in order to

---

[21] See item 226 in Chapter XX of *The Mediums' Book* by Allan Kardec [original title in French: *Le Livre des Médiums, ou, Guide des Médiums et des Évocateurs*, published in 1861], translation © 2009 by the International Spiritist Council, published in 2009 by the International Spiritist Council.

avoid danger. Emphasizing the importance of study and preparation, Kardec argues that when used with proper knowledge and precaution, mediumship is a great tool for bringing comfort, knowledge, and healing to ourselves and others. Therefore, he also provides a great deal of information for achieving safe and useful communications. For example, he explains how to understand the language of the spirits and distinguish their individual characters. He offers advice regarding the questions that should (and should not) be asked, and he informs readers about how to avoid deceptions and harmful influences. In addition, Kardec describes the Spiritist view regarding the proper role of the medium and the serious responsibility of serving as a channel of communication for the spirit realm. Finally, Kardec offers advice to the various Spiritist societies of his time, counseling them with regard to the formation and operation of a Spiritist center. This advice is still very valuable to the Spiritists of today.

Following *The Mediums' Book*, **The Gospel According to Spiritism** was published in 1864. This book explains moral maxims of Christ, illuminating them by the light of Spiritism and demonstrating their timeless moral and practical relevance to our human and spiritual life. Each chapter opens with one or more quotations from the New Testament of the Bible. Then, through the presentation of spirit communications, as well as several of Kardec's own discussions and elaborations, the various topics are explained from the perspective of Spiritist principles. These principles include immortality, spirit life, reincarnation, and evolution. Their moral significance becomes clear as they are woven throughout the different lessons. Many concepts are rescued from a literal interpretation, and the clarifications provided give them new meaning. In putting the various lessons together, we understand why we suffer, why our moral efforts and advancements are necessary to achieve happiness, and how to best engage in our relationships and interactions with others. We also find explanations of prayer, the relationships we have with brothers and sisters in the spirit realm, how to attract good spirits who can help us in positive ways, and how to avoid the influence of those who wish to steer us in the wrong direction. In this way, the lessons from Jesus come to life with clarity and logic as they are wrapped in the compassionate and motivational communications from superior spirits, combined with Kardec's supportive insights. This is why we say the book is an invaluable tool for guiding us as we navigate through the many circumstances of life, in search of true happiness. *The Gospel According to Spiritism* is an inspiration, a source of comfort, and a guide to our moral transformation.

The next book completed as part of the Spiritist codification was **Heaven and Hell**, published in 1865. Have you ever asked yourself about what really happens when we die? In the first part of this book, Kardec addresses many existing theories about the answer to this question. Putting each of them to the test of science and logic, he points out various problems left unsolved. Kardec then resolves those questions and doubts with clarifications from Spiritist teachings, and he presents the Spiritist view on what happens to the soul when leaving the material world. In this book, we learn about the experience of disconnecting from the physical body and where our souls go thereafter. We also discover how the way we are living our Earthly life will have everything to do with this future passage and what lies beyond. In addition, Kardec discusses the Spiritist view on several specific ideas that people often question, such as angels, heaven, demons, hell, purgatory, the fear of death, and Moses' prohibition against communicating with spirits. Through the combination of these different explanations, the picture of our destiny as human spirits becomes clearer, and emerging from this discussion is the Spiritist explanation of divine justice.

As a result of our exposure to this clarity and vision, many of the ideas we have held about the meaning of life undergo a transformation. For example, no longer do we fear death, for it ceases to be an unknown. Instead, we have some idea about what lies beyond – in the afterlife[22]. Likewise, we no longer fear a God who punishes. We see a loving God who educates us through laws that reflect order, compassion and fairness. In these laws, in particular the law of cause and effect, we also find a newfound motivation, courage, and calling to take charge of our own destiny.

All of these inspiring explanations comprise the first part of the book. In the second part, Kardec has put together a collection of actual spirit communications in which discarnate souls in a variety of circumstances shared their own testimonies. These include happy, average, and suffering spirits, repentant criminals, hardened spirits, and those who terminated their most recent incarnation through suicide. Here we get details about the spirits' previous lives, along with first-hand testimony about their passage from the material world and the conditions in which they subsequently found themselves in the spirit realm. These authentic narrations help to exemplify the theoretical teachings included in the first part of the text. Sometimes, one of the best ways to learn, short of personal experience, is through the example of others, and this is one case in point. Once again, we are blessed with another inspiring book.

---

[22] This is especially true when we add to Kardec's works the "Life in the Spirit World" novels written by the spirit André Luiz and psychographed by the medium Francisco Cândido Xavier.

Finally, the last book of the codification is ***Genesis***, published in 1868. If we can say that *The Gospel According to Spiritism* offers a new interpretation of biblical texts, with a moral focus, then it can be asserted that *Genesis* similarly addresses traditionally held beliefs, including religious ones, but offers a new interpretation with a scientific focus, applying Spiritist principles and revelations. To highlight some of the topics covered in the first part of the book, Kardec includes a discussion on the formation and early transformation of planet Earth. Through his explanations, it becomes clear that we do not have to think in terms of creation vs. evolution because now we can see the logical arguments for creation *through* evolution. Later in the book, Kardec talks about the subject of miracles, the so-called supernatural, and other inexplicable phenomena. He ultimately shows that such classifications are inaccurate because everything has an explanation in accordance with unchanging natural laws that regulate all of creation. The more we understand these laws, the more we and all mankind are able to identify the sources and causes of both material and spiritual phenomena. One subject that I like, in particular, is Kardec's discussion of *fluids*, which are elements of the subtle, more ethereal matter of the spiritual realm. These fluids represent the heretofore missing puzzle piece that helps us to start filling in so many gaps in our present understanding of nature.

In the latter part of *Genesis*, Kardec focuses on predictions of the gospel and a new era that is slowly coming into being, again pointing out symbolism and uniting that with the clarity of more precise teachings now brought to us by superior spirits. This is where we can find a more elaborate Spiritist explanation about the physical and moral progress our planet is undergoing. According to the spirits' teachings, the so-called "signs of the times" do indeed indicate that an end is near, but not in an apocalyptic "end of the world" way. Instead, the Earth is approaching the end of one more evolutionary stage as it transitions into the next one. When it reaches that next stage, the chaos we presently find around us will subside. Inevitably, though not without the contribution of our own efforts, this world will become a better place to live, at least for all who are deserving of the opportunity to call it home. Overall, by showing us such logical explanations, removing the clouds of mystery and magical interpretation, and pointing out the intended symbolic meaning of what has been mistakenly understood in a literal sense, *Genesis* does not, in any way, discredit the divine nature. It only restores our faith in a higher power by revealing, with a newfound clarity, the precise degree of order and perfection that permeates through all of God's creation.

Each of the last four books builds and expands upon principles outlined in the cornerstone piece, i.e. *The Spirits' Book*, thereby increasing the breadth and depth of the Spiritist base. Together, these works form a solid foundation for spiritual enlightenment. The body of knowledge that we presently know as Spiritism, including important complementary works that are fully aligned with Kardec's publications, serves as a powerful resource for students who seek a greater knowledge about the origin, nature, meaning, and destiny of life.

7
A Holistic View

No matter how long I continue to study Spiritism, I'm always amazed by its holistic view of life. It seems that each new Spiritist book I've ever read has only added a layer of depth to this fascinating discovery. For starters, one of the most valuable characteristics of Spiritism is that which we refer to as its *triple aspect*. This denotes the comprehensive scope of Spiritism and the revealing synergy of its scientific, philosophic, and religious or moral aspects. If we remove any one of those, we're no longer talking about Spiritism as codified by Allan Kardec.

As a newcomer to Spiritism several years ago, I found it very refreshing to read Kardec's statements in *The Gospel According to Spiritism* about the need for an alignment between science and religion.[23] No doubt, many would agree that if science and religion were to walk hand in hand, it would make life a lot less confusing! Yet, how can this be achieved when opposing fundamentals create a perpetual barrier between the two? This is where Spiritism comes to the rescue. First, it acknowledges and explains our existence as spirits. Second, it admits the evolutionary nature of human knowledge. Spiritism recognizes that this knowledge includes not only the material elements of this world, as studied by our physical sciences, but the spiritual ones as well. Does this mean that God changes things around on us? No, it doesn't; both God and the natural laws that govern creation are eternal and unchanging. What changes is our understanding, which gains both breadth and depth as we evolve and mature. Just as a small child, a teenager, and an experienced adult

---

[23] See Chapter 1 "A Personal Message".

will typically have very different views of the world, so, too, do spirits at varying progressive levels of spiritual development.

The scientific aspect of Spiritism began with Allan Kardec's careful observance of spirit phenomena. This was primarily "rapping" and "table turning", manifestations commonly cited as representing the beginnings of the nineteenth-century *spiritualist* movement. This was followed by Kardec's rigorous study of numerous communications received from discarnate spirits[24], that is, once he discovered them to be the cause of those physical phenomena. Most observers, at the time, had simply found the manifestations to be entertaining at best. However, this was the way that spirits of a lower order had been carrying out their task of getting man's attention. In doing so, they made way for more evolved and illuminated spirits to come and bring forth the various elements of the Spiritist teachings. Allan Kardec was the one called to the task of making these teachings available to everyone, and he was, indeed, the right man for this very important work. Kardec was a highly educated and morally upright person with a healthy degree of skepticism and a tremendous sense of logic and reason. Likewise, he had both the capacity and willingness to exercise due diligence necessary to ensure a meticulous, systematic study of these communications, which were collected in their entirety from spirits representing all stages of development.

Within the gems of information collected from these spirits came new revelations, specifically from spirits of a higher order, concerning details about our spiritual nature and makeup, as well as the world in which we live. These details had both a scientific and philosophical character. They

---

[24] These communications were received through the collaboration of mediums, including ones that Kardec worked with directly and other mediums around the world.

also made clear the existence of moral consequences associated with our actions. From a scientific standpoint, Kardec had found compelling evidence for the existence of the soul, its survival after the death of the physical body, and its ability to communicate with those still living on Earth. It's worth noting that all this happened before the development of more recent scientific studies with which we are familiar, such as those of past-life regression, near-death experiences, spontaneous past-life memories (in adults and children), and the study of brain activity during the exercise of mediumship, all of which provide further evidence to support those earlier discoveries. That said, the scope of those scientific details revealed to Kardec went far beyond just the immortality and communicability of the spirits. Through them, we learn about basic elements of the universe explained like you've probably never heard. These elements formed the basis for further explanations on topics such as the character and attributes of spirits; the perispirit[25] and how it relates to both the immaterial soul and the purely material body; mediumship and how it actually works; and so much more.

Pedro Barbosa, a Spiritist author, once wrote, "Thanks to scientific Spiritism, the ancient, antagonistic divide between science and faith disappears because now it is no longer about the utopian spiritualism, dogmas, superstitions, the supernatural, or the mystic."[26] Indeed, the scientific aspects of Spiritism, in combination with the philosophic and moral aspects, comprise the puzzle pieces that will allow mankind to make great strides in advancing our traditional sciences. From biology, sociology, and geology, to astronomy,

---

[25] The perispirit was introduced in Chapter 4 "A Starting Point".

[26] Barbosa, Pedro Franco. *Espiritismo Basico* [title translation: *Basic Spiritism*"; to date, an English translation of the book has not been published.]. 3rd ed. Rio de Janeiro–RJ, Brazil: Federação Espírita Brasileira [Brazilian Spiritist Federation].1987. pg 105.

psychology, physics, etc., a new world will open as scientists discover our spiritual reality. We are making small steps in this direction, but someday we will be, collectively, at a point where Spiritism has been for over 150 years.

I have included in this chapter more detail about the scientific aspect of Spiritism than the philosophical and moral aspects, which will be the primary focus of the remainder of this book. That said, nearly all points in the philosophical and moral aspects are, in fact, supported and further explained by details we could classify under the scientific category. In a perfectly holistic way, the lines through which we make these divisions are not exactly black and white, but talking about each of the three aspects helps us to understand the extent of this knowledge in its totality. To keep from overextending this book in length or complexity, I will leave the scientific aspect, with the exception of an occasional mention, for you to explore later on in a more elaborate study of Spiritism.

The philosophical foundation of Spiritism was also derived from information gathered through communication with discarnate spirits, as well as Kardec's careful study of the same and the efforts he made to explain it to us in a way we could understand and use. Among other things, these philosophical aspects include details regarding spirit life and the journey of evolution through the process of reincarnation. A natural consequence of our increased knowledge, in this area, becomes a greater understanding of the role we play in our own spiritual evolution. I will talk more about that in a later chapter.

This philosophy helps us to understand God's natural laws which govern all life. From an ethical perspective, when considering moral evolution, Spiritists study the lessons and examples of Jesus as our model and guide, and we make efforts to practice what he taught. We also appreciate the seeds of universal moral truth that have surfaced throughout time in various philosophies and religions around the world. These truths reflect elements of the ethical principles most relevant and most pertinent to our eventual attainment of true purification and happiness. We can then "consider the Spiritist Doctrine in its religious aspect when it establishes a moral tie between men, leading them in the direction of the Creator, through the application of the moral teachings of Christ."[27]

My comments on this subject will end here. While I can offer this high-level explanation, you will appreciate it more after you delve into what lies below the surface. In putting all these elements together, we no longer see one aspect of life in isolation from another. As Kardec wrote, Spiritism "joins into a whole what has been scattered"[28]. The beauty of this holistic approach lies in what we are able to take from and do with this new picture that becomes clearer as we continue to study Spiritism.

---

[27] Brazilian Spiritist Federation in its educational text *Systematic Study of Spiritism*, published in 1996, Program #1, Section # 6. (published in Portuguese).

[28] See Allan Kardec's conclusion to *The Spirits' Book*, part VI [original title in French: *Le Livre des Espirits*, published in 1857 with 2nd edition in 1860], translation © 2006 by the International Spiritist Council, authorized edition printed in 2010 by Edicei of America.

8
Life and Love Are Not Lost

One of the most consoling lessons among those that Kardec derived from his judicious studies of spiritual phenomena and spirit communications is that life is simply not over when this material existence comes to an end. To the same degree, we learn that the bonds of love and affection that we establish with one another are not severed by the grave. Instead, we go on, and our connections of the heart are lasting. Both life and love are eternal.

What a relief it is to have this consoling certainty! The fact that life goes on is a message I want to express loud and clear. In fact, if I could I would scream it from mountain tops and put it in neon lights. People need to know this. More than that, they need to really understand it. If I had been sure of this some years ago, it would definitely have made one particular event in my life much easier.

Of course, there are many people who already know or believe in *life after death* with every fiber in their body, and they find great comfort in it. Likewise, among all who do *not* believe that life goes on, I don't think there's one who doesn't realize how many other people do believe. This is not a new concept. However, many people have doubts – from the completely skeptical to those who would just like to feel more confident than they do. I know. I was once among them. My grandfather passed away when I was in my early 20s, and I didn't handle it well. To be honest, I was an emotional mess. I had this reaction even though my grandfather was relatively older and had lived a very good life, leaving behind great memories for the rest of us to cherish. In contrast, there are people "dying" every day after experiencing lives that were nothing but struggle or that seemed (when seen only from the surface) to be unfairly short-lived. Circumstances like those make for an even more difficult experience for the survivors.

In any case, for those who live with doubt, to face the passing of a loved one can be one of the most painful of life experiences. For this reason, it is such a comforting relief to find that death does **not** "do us part", and the elimination of this doubt is potentially *life changing*. Spiritism is one source of such relief. It has delivered exceptional evidence for the existence and survival of the soul, the foundation of which we owe to the vision, discipline, and astuteness of Allan Kardec. This finding is such a source of comfort that even if it were the single contribution that Spiritism ever made to mankind, it would be extremely valuable.

As I have alluded to in this book, Spiritism's overall contribution goes far beyond validating this basic notion. One closely related example is the insight Spiritism provides regarding what happens once we leave this material existence. Everyone wants to know if our loved ones are still around us, thinking about us, and what the afterlife is like. In a subsequent chapter, I discuss how Spiritism illustrates that it is not just that the soul stays *alive* but that it truly goes on *living*. Furthermore, Spiritism puts to rest the idea of eternal punishment and other related misconceptions; it shows that no matter what our situation upon returning to the spirit realm, there will always come a day when we will again see all of those for whom we hold great affection. We'll also be reunited, in great harmony, with those with whom we haven't always seen eye-to-eye. The process of reincarnation, imbued with the compassion of God, is what gives this awesome confidence in what, without it, may have only seemed like a dream.

This belief in the survival of the soul gives rise to something else worth considering. That is the way we talk about death. I've found that when we need to give our condolences to others who are dealing with the immediacy of a loved one's passing, we have a tendency to make statements like "I'm sorry for your loss." Even with my knowledge from Spiritism, I know that it's hard to find the words to say in these moments. What you really wish you could do is say something that would ease the other person's pain or express how much you sympathize with him or her. I definitely understand that this kind of remark truly comes from the heart. However, I believe that we now need to reflect on the message we are giving or the kind of idea that we are, even involuntarily, perpetuating with such words. The truth is that while we become temporarily separated from those who pass before us (in terms of who we can see, hear, and touch), those individuals are never actually *lost*, and this is the mindset we need to change. In addition, as painful as that separation can be, perhaps referring to it as if it were permanent only sustains a negative way of thinking and feeling. This is even more significant when we consider that our discarnate loved ones do not want to see us in inconsolable grief; such a reaction on our part actually causes them suffering and makes *their* separation process more difficult. Again, it's not easy to find the words, but let's reflect on these ideas and try to console others with comforting words, such as commenting about how special the one who passed is and letting those left behind know that we are praying for them.

◊ ◊ ◊

I encourage you to reflect on *your* beliefs about death. Do you have any of the same doubts I once had? Do you question what happens with those who seem to be taken away from us? Do you wonder what the purpose could be of all the experiences we have and the relationships we build if one day it's all over? If you do have such questions, then I strongly encourage you to look into Spiritism. I'd also like you to ponder one last thought. Consider for a moment how we typically rejoice and celebrate when a new baby comes into this world, but we feel sad when the time comes for a loved one to leave, regardless of our particular beliefs. Well, in the spirit realm, just the opposite happens. A new life on Earth requires a kind of temporary separation from the ones left behind in the spirit realm. Meanwhile, when the spirit who had incarnated eventually returns to the spirit world, the loved ones rejoice and celebrate the reunion. Imagine our spiritual existence taking place in a big space with a revolving door in the middle. On one side is the spirit world, and on the other is the material world. At any given time, some are coming while others are going. We all travel back and forth in a perfectly natural way, and there's always a reason behind each trip we make from one side to the other. The more we understand this, the easier it will become to accept the changes resulting from a loved one's disincarnation, and the more we will trust in God's wisdom to know exactly what is right for us in each moment.

9
Spirits: Seen and Heard, but Too Seldom Mentioned

This brief chapter is mostly a personal contemplation of my own. I felt it was worth sharing for the benefit of those who can relate to my experience. Ultimately, it is my hope that after reading this and subsequent chapters, you will perceive more clearly the kind of transforming effect Spiritism can have on one's perspective. In addition, there is a point that I want to make based on the reflection I will now share.

In thinking about my childhood and youth, I do not recall any serious talk – in my home, at my school, among my family members, with my friends, or in any other setting I can think of – about spirits. It was just a subject that never came up. Of course, I'd heard of ghosts, haunted houses, and the like, but I thought of them as something factitious or derived from fantasy. I'd heard the terms soul, everlasting soul, and immortal soul, but never did I hear them used, or the actual word, *spirit*, spoken with the depth and scope of meaning that the same term has in Spiritism. I'd heard of spirits in the sense of warding off evil spirits, but I never heard of attracting good spirits. I certainly never was told that I *was* a spirit! The closest I ever came to thinking about good spirits, or considering myself to be a spirit, was when I dressed up one year as Casper the Friendly Ghost for Halloween, which I find funny now because my mother says this was the only way I would dress like a ghost at all. I recall trying once to play with an Ouija board, but if I remember correctly, we didn't get it to work; thank goodness. I do remember learning about our Native Americans' belief in their ancestral spirits, and I found it intriguing, but I suppose I simply attributed that and other similar beliefs to cultural tradition.

Finally, I had no idea how many famous people in history have had a belief in spirits or even in subjects like reincarnation. I certainly had no knowledge of the spiritualist activity and the table-turning phenomena of the 1800s, or of the scientific research that was done regarding spirits, back in the 1800s and early 1900s. If you are familiar with the history of Spiritualism, you may understand why I find it so amusing that I actually grew up in upstate NY less than 40 miles from the little hamlet of Hydesville. This location is considered to be the birthplace of nineteenth-century Spiritualism. Ironically, I'd never heard of it until later in life when, living over a thousand miles away, I began to study Spiritism.

Looking back now, I can see I was quite naïve about this subject. I recognize this, and I know that aside from the spiritualist movement and the scientific studies conducted in recent eras, a belief in spirits, or perhaps I should say knowledge of them, has been present throughout history and in nearly every place, culture, or belief system. In hindsight, I'm actually surprised that when I was younger, I never gave more thought to the idea of spirits, ghosts, or the fact that people claimed to see and hear them. I know I was not alone. In fairness to myself and others, we did not then have the same access or exposure to the information now found in television, the internet, books, and other resources. Even now, however, I know there are still many people who don't give it much consideration. Although this is changing ever more quickly, our society in general still seems to feel skeptical or fearful when it comes to spirits. I think this is why people often feel a bit sheepish about the word *Spiritism* when they first hear of it. I cannot blame them. I once felt that way myself! I do realize that there are many sources of misinformation that have people quite confused about spirits. For these reasons, the Spiritist movement is working to combat such misunderstandings by sharing the insights and clarifications derived from the Spiritist body of knowledge.

I occasionally hear about individuals who have experienced paranormal phenomenon but have refrained from telling others, as they fear being ridiculed or accused of being mistaken. I suspect that living among us there are many people just like them who've preferred to remain silent. Aside from this, I am learning about the growing number of individuals who either believe in or are open to the idea of reincarnation but are shy about bringing their views, interests, or questions into open conversation.

We need to change all this. Spirits, the spirit world, and our communications and interactions with the spiritual realm, as well as the multiplicity of lives and the plurality of worlds, are all very natural parts of our reality. It is time for this understanding, with all due clarifications and explanations, to become common knowledge. I am reminded of a quotation from Allan Kardec, in the prologue to *The Spirits' Book*, where he writes:

> "The Spirits have announced that the time appointed by Providence for a universal manifestation has now come, and that as ministers of God and agents of the divine will, their mission is to instruct and enlighten men and women, opening a new era for the regeneration of humankind. This book is a compilation of their teachings. It has been written at the order and under the dictation of high order spirits, in order to establish the basis of a rational philosophy free from prejudices of preconceived notions."

Spiritism is a treasure chest of wisdom, holding gems that have been passed down over centuries. At various points throughout history, including that of the codification of

Spiritism, these gems have been polished so as to progressively reveal their true beauty. We must now take the gold and the diamonds out of the chest and let them shine all over the world, giving everyone the opportunity to feel enriched by this abundance of truth.

10
Life After Death and The Spirit World: Wow!

When it comes to spirituality, one of the common topics we find people longing to know more about is life after death. Certainly, there are many people who believe that life does not end at the grave. At the same time, there are many who feel they have no reason to believe in the soul or its survival of the body. Some, quite frankly, just don't know what to believe. What many newcomers to Spiritism find so surprising is not just that life, indeed, goes on, but that it goes on in a very real and active way. This is quite a significant shift in thinking for many.

Perhaps you have read the Spiritist book *Nosso Lar*, written by the spirit author André Luiz[29] and psychographed by the medium Francisco Cândido Xavier[30]. Or maybe you've seen *Astral City: A Spiritual Journey*[31], the movie recently produced based on this novel. If you had no prior knowledge about Spiritism, or if you were unaware of the heart, soul, and

---

[29] You will read more about André Luiz later in this chapter.

[30] The Brazilian medium Francisco Cândido Xavier, also known as "Chico" Xavier (1910 – 2002), was a prominent 20th-century contributor to the Spiritist movement. Xavier's highly ostensive mediumistic faculty, through which Xavier exhibited great mediumistic abilities, as well as many forms of mediumship, was a substantial factor in his ability to facilitate the manifestation of spiritual beings in the material realm. No less significant to the Spiritist movement was Xavier's moral character, one of exemplary humility, simplicity, and faith. Xavier demonstrated admirable perseverance and discipline, in addition to a deep love for humanity. Xavier psychographed over 400 books, a great many of which now represent renowned publications among the works of Spiritist literature. In demonstration of Xavier's humility and generosity, all proceeds from the sale of those books were donated to charity. For further details, I recommend the video about Xavier shared at ExploreSpiritism.com/historychicoxavier.htm.

[31] This is the title as translated for distribution in English-speaking countries. The original movie title in Portuguese was *Nosso Lar*.

selfless work of this beloved medium, also known by his nickname, Chico Xavier, you might think the details of this book came right out of science fiction. We're talking spiritual cities, organized with buildings, departments and ministries, as well as places to heal, work, live, and study! However, it is a true story, and that's what I mean by a shift in thinking. After all, it's one thing to believe in life after death, quite another to have knowledge about what that life is actually like, and still yet another to understand how the discarnate beings in that *after death* state interact with those still living in the material world. Aside from being comforting and enlightening, Spiritism educates us with an awareness of all three of these areas of knowledge. In doing so, it helps us make better decisions in our lives.

Once in a while, you may hear someone say that we don't know what it's like *on the other side* because no one has been able to come back to tell us. Well, that's simply not the case. Our discarnate brothers and sisters have indeed been able to share such information with us at different times and places throughout history. We owe this blessing to the faculty of mediumship, which has allowed those spirits to communicate to us through mediums around the world. In this way, humanity has received information from spirits of all different categories[32]. Some have merely shared their own feelings and experiences, while others have displayed a more advanced level of knowledge. In all cases, they have allowed us to gain a broader perspective.[33]

This form of communication is not limited to, nor did it originate in Spiritism. However, what we find in Spiritism

---

[32] These categories refer to factors such as their living condition at the time, state of mind and temperament, degree of moral and intellectual advancement, etc.

[33] This knowledge has been acquired through their own process of evolution.

is the result of Kardec's dedicated and organized work. In putting countless spirit communications through a number of careful analyses, Kardec then identified reliable sources of information and pinpointed the areas of universal agreement among them. Subsequent to the content of Kardec's books, we find further details provided through the collaborative work of mediums. These include both firsthand and third party accounts shared by entities in the spirit realm. Such intriguing details help to paint in the colors and bring to life the outlines so carefully traced throughout the works of Kardec and his collaborators. Furthermore, unlike the elitist, spiritual wisdom, once so closely guarded by a select few, Spiritism purposefully makes this knowledge widely available.

In Spiritism, we refer to the *other side* as the spirit(ual) realm or world. This is not merely our destination after life on Earth. It is actually the home we parted from in coming here. The spirit realm is another dimension that co-exists with the material one. For us, as immortal spirits, it is our true home. In other words, we spend most of our time in the spirit realm and leave only for short intervals that offer us opportunities important to our evolutionary process.[34] We use the term, *discarnate,* to describe those living in the spirit realm and the term, *incarnate,* to describe the embodied souls living in the material world (meaning you and me). Learning and growing takes place in both worlds. However, there are certain experiences created by the necessities inherent to the material life that make our incarnation in the material world necessary for our spiritual development.

In Kardec's books, starting with *The Spirits' Book*, we begin to better understand the nature of spirits as we learn

---

[34] These intervals become the temporary lifetimes that we have in the material world.

about certain characteristics attributed to them. We also find enlightening details concerning life in the spirit realm. In *The Mediums' Book*, we learn more about how spirits can make their presence known in the material world as well as how they communicate with us through mediumship. While the power of thought and the law of attraction are certainly popular topics nowadays, one of the chapters in *Genesis* explains just how our thoughts become the means of interacting with and taking part in creating our spiritual environment. In *Heaven and Hell*, we find further explanation of life after death. In particular, we see how the use of our free will and the way we live our lives will affect our experiences upon returning once again to inhabit the spirit realm. Finally, *The Gospel According to Spiritism* elaborates on important moral teachings, guiding us through the ethical maze of life on Earth. In doing so, it empowers us to live our lives in such a way that we will find ourselves rewarded by a peaceful conscience when this lifetime comes to an end.

Aside from Kardec's books, there are many others that elaborate on these topics and aid in our understanding of such concepts. For example, the renowned early nineteenth-century apostle of Spiritism, Léon Denis[35], describes the variety of conditions, sights, sounds, and sensations experienced by those inhabiting the spirit realm with such eloquence that his

---

[35] Following Spiritism's codification by Allan Kardec, one of its most prominent disseminators was another Frenchman, Léon Denis. Denis is often referred to as the Consolidator, or Apostle, of Spiritism. He lived during approximately the same time period as Allan Kardec (Kardec 1804-1869, Denis 1846-1927). Denis took great interest in Spiritism from the moment he discovered *The Spirits' Book* at age 18. Later, through his inspirational speaking and writing, Denis dedicated himself to Spiritism's dissemination, including the continuation of mediumistic research, the promotion of the Spiritist movement in France, and the deep exploration of the moral aspect of Spiritism. You can read more about Denis at the webpage, ExploreSpiritism.com/historyleondenis.htm

writing becomes both enchanting and illuminating.[36] His descriptions of the blissful environments, sublime sentiments, and surroundings of wondrous beauty enjoyed by the most deserving of souls leave one longing, hopeful, and inspired to earn the merit required for such a rewarding life. Meanwhile, he creates for us an illustrative and meaningful visual of the harshness, the shadows, and the darkness experienced by those souls tormented by their own conscience. In between these extremes, there is a great spectrum of environments, which Denis, likewise, does not fail to explain.

True to the Spiritist message of hope and progress, Denis also demonstrates that God is always just. For example, he explains that no one is exempt from those harsh realities that are at times the remedy required to heal ailing souls who suffer from detriments of their own creation. At the same time, however, he makes it clear that the contrasting, well-deserved, and glorious splendor is just as much available to each and every one of us provided we make the efforts to progress to such levels. Each positive step we make will bring us more enjoyable experiences, not only in the spirit world but in the numerous material worlds, as well.

Another excellent resource for learning more about the spirit world is the series of true-story novels written by the spirit author André Luiz, through the medium Francisco Cândido Xavier. The celebrated book I mentioned earlier, *Nosso Lar*, was the first novel in this series. The spirit known as André Luiz was a medical doctor and researcher on Earth in the early twentieth century. His return to the spirit realm and subsequent awakening in that state marked the beginning of a new journey through a number of intriguing

---

[36] See *Here and Hereafter* [original title in French: *Aprés La Mort*, published in 1889], translation to English by George G. Fleurot in 1909, as printed in 2005 by the Spiritist Alliance for Books.

experiences which were all at once transforming and educational. With time, André had the opportunity to travel to many places accompanied by spiritual friends and instructors. He was able to observe several different aspects of spirit life, including unfolding, formative events that were part of the lives of other spirits in both the material and spiritual worlds.

Those learning experiences and André's narration of them form the basis for many different novels that came to follow, consequently earning André Luiz the reputation among Spiritists as not only a reporter from the spirit realm, but also a beloved friend and highly appreciated contributor to humankind's awareness of our spiritual reality. The lessons woven throughout these novels are remarkably in sync with the teachings found throughout the codification of Spiritism. In fact, they bring those teachings to life with elucidating examples, descriptions, and accounts.

◊ ◊ ◊

One thing that becomes very clear in Spiritism is that to describe the living conditions of any given spirit in the spirit realm, we must first ask what that spirit is like, in terms of its thoughts, behaviors, desires, interests, and tendencies. Through the law of attraction, and by the workings of the conscience, discarnate spirits are naturally drawn to the places and conditions with which they have an affinity. We say that in death we leave behind the physical body. This means that our spirits disconnect from that material garment which served as the gear capable of facilitating our interaction with the material world. However, this transition alone does not change us from who we were just before that disconnection, meaning our personality and beliefs, the objects of our attention, and the kinds of thoughts and behaviors we cultivated on Earth. In particular, we will demonstrate the same spiritual and mental states prevalent before our disincarnation.

Once we do make the transition, those defining aspects of our personality will shape our experiences as we reencounter the spiritual world. Think, for a moment, about the great variety of characters we find among those living on Earth. Even more diverse are the discarnate beings living throughout creation. According to Spiritism, the environments of the spiritual realm reflect the quality of thoughts cultivated by their inhabitants. Therefore, Spiritist teachings reveal an extensive degree of diversity among the many dwelling places of the spiritual world.

Notwithstanding those places so majestic and sublime, what about the environments closer to our present stage of evolution yet reachable through morally sound behavior and regular efforts to change oneself for the better? What kinds of places are these, and what is life like there? For those who have read *Nosso Lar* or have seen the aforementioned movie based on that book, the spiritual city that is the primary setting for the novel is one example. In such places, life continues, and the spirits remain active. In general, there is an organized way of living with enjoyable surroundings. In some cases, there are pleasant elements of nature, music, art, and technology still unknown to us on Earth. There are opportunities to grow through study, worship, and numerous forms of work carried out to benefit others. Spirits in such places live in the company of loved ones and others with whom they share an affinity. Likewise, when merited and appropriate, they may keep watch over and help loved ones incarnated in the material world. When permitted, there are chances to review details of one's spiritual past and reflect on what kinds of experiences would be desired for a future incarnation. This description paints a general picture, but you get the idea. If you think this sounds quite like Earth, but better, that's because such a comparison is actually quite accurate!

In contrast to the above, not every place or experience in the spirit realm is so enjoyable. In fact, there is no shortage of souls who suffer, though it's important to reiterate that this is never a permanent condition. Among the less pleasant experiences, there are varieties that can emerge but are overcome much more quickly, such as confusion or initial difficulty in readapting. This is influenced, in part, by the way one understands or thinks about this transition prior to actually making it. However, barring any special circumstances, it will subside as one receives assistance in understanding the new situation.

Not all the unpleasant conditions are short lived. In general, it is our mental and emotional states, as well as the thoughts we nurture, that will determine the places and environments we are attracted to. Therefore, when these are persistently negative, they result in more lasting forms of suffering. In other words, heavier vibrations formed through the negative thoughts and energies we emit can create corresponding degrees of darkness and shadow around us. For example, we can experience guilt or remorse over how we acted, what we did or failed to do, the choices we made, or the hurt we may have caused during our most recent time in the material world. While the remorse is painful, it is also the necessary first step toward healing and reparation. However, if we continue cultivating lamentably inferior thoughts and vibrations, these can blind us from such a vision of our past. They may even lead us to continue in our backward ways, thus aggravating our condition.

In other unfortunate circumstances, we may have suffered on Earth from an addiction to harmful substances or unhealthy behaviors. If we did not overcome such an addiction before leaving the material world, our desire to satisfy those dependencies will continue to pervade our thoughts after our return to the spirit realm. Furthermore, there's a lamentable form of suffering caused by a pattern of inferior and harmful feelings, like anger, resentment, hatred, and the like. When we carry these emotions with us and hang onto them as we return to the spirit world, we consequently perpetuate the harm they cause. This should not come as a surprise; it is no different from life on Earth, where the difficulty to tolerate, understand, and forgive results in the stubborn harboring of such sentiments. Indeed, this hardness of the heart may hurt the individual targeted by such thoughts. However, the ultimate prisoner is the one who carries them. At some point, we will always have to let go and learn to forgive. This is why teachings about forgiveness, including forgiveness of others and of ourselves, are so important. The sooner we forgive, the less suffering we inevitably endure as a result.

Aside from the surprise of discovering just how actively discarnate spirits live in the spirit realm, another surprising revelation from Spiritism is how the spiritual and material worlds regularly interact with one another. They do not operate in isolation as one might think. For instance, there are moments when we, as incarnate spirits, spend time in the spirit world. One example is when our souls become partially liberated from our physical bodies during sleep. During those times, the law of attraction determines the places and beings we visit, in the same way that it does for fully discarnate spirits. For example, we may take part in activities that we enjoy, visit with loved ones, get advice from our spiritual mentors, receive healing treatments, or work in benefit of others. In addition, there are numerous ways in which spirits from the spirit realm influence those of us living on Earth. You will find some examples of this in other chapters of this book. It is truly fascinating when we come to realize just how much they are a part of our lives from the beginning to the end.

If you want to know more about this, I highly recommend the books from André Luiz's "Life in the Spirit Word" series. The captivating accounts shared in these books provide great lessons found in the comments and explanations from spiritual instructors involved in André's various learning experiences. Even more so, they provide readers with powerful visualizations demonstrating how the theoretical concepts of Spiritism actually play out in real life situations. Such descriptions and visuals become a great tool for us, enabling us to better imagine the influence of spirits, past lives, and the like, in our present material lives. There are several different novels in the series. Each focuses on a different aspect of spiritual or material life. Through this collection, we find illustrations of the realities of life in the spirit world and the mutual influence between our two realms. We discover the spiritual ties and webs of "inter-incarnatory" relationships through which we weave the chapters of our stories as immortal spirits. We also learn about the tireless dedication and love from spiritual benefactors, who work in God's name to bring comfort, aid, knowledge, and support to those in need, including both incarnate and discarnate spirits. Finally, we better understand the infallible, compassionate justice of our Creator.

Spiritism has so much to teach us about the continuity of our immortal existence. No longer do we have to question what to expect when our life on Earth comes to an end. For the soul, that time simply represents a new beginning. We do not have to live with fear of the unknown or with false notions that instill despair. It is time for new perspectives. We now have a great deal of information available to us about life after death, or better, life after life. Ultimately, these revelations illustrate the grand significance of how we choose to live our lives in the material world. They are, at once, fascinating, enlightening, and inspiring. After reading these books and reflecting on the significance of their lessons, it is almost impossible not to see life in a new way.

11
Reincarnation, Evolution, and Free Will

If you would have asked me fifteen or twenty years ago what I thought about reincarnation, I would have probably referred to it as a religious belief some people embraced but one to which I did not adhere. Growing up, I had very little exposure to the idea of reincarnation. Most of what I'd learned came from a brief introduction in one of my high school classes. I sometimes joke now that for all we heard in school about Benjamin Franklin, Thomas Edison, Henry Ford, and others, we surely never heard about their belief in reincarnation. Likewise, when sitting in high school geometry class and learning about the famous Pythagorean Theorem, I never imagined that its discoverer was also a spiritual leader of his day who believed in the multiplicity of lives. Actually, I really had no idea how wide-spread the concept or belief was or the extent of its roots in history. I'm not saying my case is the same as that of everyone around me, but I know that I am, by far, not alone. Of course I cannot generalize; however, it is my personal perception that until recently and especially in the Western culture, many people have had only a vague impression on the topic or have tended to think of it as a mere relic of ancient cultures.

Fortunately, this is changing. In recent years, much evidence for the existence of reincarnation has surfaced in fields of scientific research. This includes findings from past-life regressions induced by hypnotherapy, spontaneous past-life memories in adults (who have also become more willing to disclose them), and perhaps the most credible evidence of all – the spontaneous past-life memories of children. These children talk about places, times, and even particular people that they would have never known about otherwise.

In places and cultures where reincarnation is not a commonly held belief, this evidence is slowly bringing about a general awakening, thus opening minds to the possibility that we can or do really live more than just one life. For those who reach this point as a result of such findings, but do not necessarily subscribe to the particular teachings of traditional belief systems that include reincarnation, many questions may arise. They may be left wondering what this reality means for us, whether the process ever ends, where we go between incarnations, or why we can't remember our past lives. They may also question how they can reconcile such knowledge with what they've always believed about life, death, and our Creator.

Spiritism answers those questions. However, it does not teach us about reincarnation as a system of religious dogma. Instead, it illustrates why reincarnation represents the compassionate nature of God and, quite importantly, it brings us to realize the direct role that we have in the way our spiritual journey plays out over time.

One thing that becomes progressively clearer as one continues to study Spiritism is that we are part of a creation in which everything in existence comes together in a perfect order, directed and harmonized by the laws of nature, or divine laws. These include both physical, as well as moral laws. Every human spirit is created in what we refer to as a state of simplicity and unawareness, destined to follow an evolutionary path of progress. This includes intellectual progress, referring to the capacity of our intellect, understanding, and reason, as well as moral progress, meaning the development of our ethical sense, a cultivation of moral virtues, and above all, a growing ability to love.

So how exactly does this progress work? At the beginning of this journey, a spirit has very little free will, meaning the capability and means by which to take conscious, deliberate action. Instead, the spirit acts primarily based on instinct. However, through a series of experiences and over the course of multiple lifetimes, the spirit's level of knowledge and its awareness of both itself and of the world around it grows. Just think about the most primitive era of human life on Earth. Picture the most elementary human life form you can imagine. Now look at how we live today. Look at the advancements that have been made in the sciences and the arts. This trend reflects the overall evolutionary progress of our planet. Aside from this general progress, we also find some individuals who are extremely knowledgeable and talented; some are so advanced, almost from the time of birth, that we call them prodigies. Meanwhile, alongside them, we find others who are far less advanced in these areas. The entirety of differences between them results from the varying degrees of progress found among Earth's inhabitants.

Morally speaking, consider the fact that there was a time when man had to be told not to murder, lie, or steal. Yes, several today are still learning those lessons, but you cannot deny that such a notion is rather intuitive for most people. Meanwhile, still other individuals live exemplary lives, demonstrating a tremendous, innate sense of compassion, justice, and selflessness. Of course, we find a gazillion shades in between these classifications, all representing different stages of personal progress.

I need to clarify that, as spirits, we are able to advance in this way and continuously build on our past experiences. Instead of being re-absorbed, so to speak, by the source from which we came, we will actually maintain our individuality throughout this sequence of lifetimes, as well as in between each of them. Nothing is lost! As already discussed, death does not really exist, with the exception of the perishing physical body that we leave behind at the end of each material lifetime. After that, we return to the spirit realm, our true home, where we actually spend most of our time.

As our spirits progress through a series of multiple material lives, or incarnations, and we achieve new levels of growth, we also earn greater levels of free will. This means that we have a greater liberty to make choices. However, this free will calls on us to use our ever-maturing ability to reason, as well as our developing sense of right and wrong, i.e., the emerging inner voice of our conscience. Therefore, just as important as this ever-growing allowance of free will is the fact that with it comes a corresponding degree of responsibility and accountability for our actions. When we use our free will to make good choices, ones that are in agreement with the moral laws of nature, we will achieve progress and thereby earn merit for future rewards. What kinds of rewards are those? They include: better conditions in future lifetimes, pleasant conditions upon returning to the spirit realm, greater merit for the company of and assistance from good spirits, happiness that comes from living our lives with a healthy perspective, the joy of meaningful relationships (which death cannot destroy), and one thing that cannot be underrated – the peace achieved by being in harmony with one's own conscience.

To the contrary, when we make poor choices, ones that cause harm to ourselves or to others, we become indebted to the law and to our fellow beings. In this way, we acquire disturbances of the conscience that will sooner or later bring about the pain of remorse. These events become a cause for delay in our spiritual progress. We will often begin to experience the consequences of poor choices during the same lifetime in which we made them. If we do not awaken to this accountability or make the necessary readjustments before this lifetime ends, we will return to the spirit realm with unresolved debts and lessons yet to be learned.

What's important to know is that our Creator always allows us the opportunity to redeem ourselves and get back on track. There is no such thing as eternal damnation or punishment. In fact, God does not actually punish us at all. Instead, divine laws serve to educate us and bring about our progress. From the spirit realm, once we take account of how we spent our time on Earth, we review all the good we did, as well as all the wrong, and we acknowledge any debts we have acquired. Then, it is our own conscience which directs us to accept and even ask for new opportunities that can facilitate relief from our remorseful conscience, thus enabling our return to the pathway of knowledge and love. This is how the process of reincarnation actually represents a divine blessing.

Through reincarnation, we can return to the material life and reunite with individuals from our past in order to help those whom we hurt, uplift those whom we belittled, correct what we have done wrong, give value to something or someone that we may have failed to appreciate, and so on. Just the same, there are also times when we come to forgive those who have hurt us. We can even come to live alongside loved ones and help them through difficult trials.

The hardships that we undergo in this process offer valuable lessons while serving as remedies that help treat and purify our souls. These pains and struggles can take all shapes and forms, such as difficult relationships, arduous living conditions, significant losses or disappointments, painful treatment by others, and various forms of mental and physical illness or challenges. All have a purpose. Spiritism makes us aware of why we must do our best to endure them with patience, resignation, and courage, and in the depths of its teachings and examples, it gives us the tools for doing so.

These tools also help us to reach greater levels of progress. Our objectives in life are not limited to paying off debts from our past. Life is also about creating our future according to how we make use of our free will today. Therefore, we also encounter numerous opportunities to earn new merits, to step out of the shadows of our past, and to walk toward the better and brighter future that lies before each and every one of us. We will do so by making the effort to cultivate healthy thoughts, a more upright conduct, and more noble sentiments. This illustrates why reincarnation according to Spiritism is always associated with progressive evolution. We may stagnate, delay, or reveal signs that we are not quite as advanced as we thought, but we never regress.

Because of the privilege and responsibility of our free will, we say that our progress requires *conscious* growth. It is precisely by understanding concepts such as the continuity of life, the opportunity we have to exercise our free will, the mechanisms of cause and effect, and the action of various natural laws that we begin to explain the otherwise inexplicable. We can now answer questions such as these: Why is there so much disparity between the traits and characteristics of people? Why are we born into such a wide variety of circumstances? Why do bad things happen to good people? Why do good people do bad things?

Do not believe that Spiritism teaches all of this as mere theoretical concepts. It offers specific examples, as well. In certain Spiritist books, you will find personal testimonies from discarnate spirits who share their own experiences, as well as narrations told by other spirits who document the stories of their fellow beings in both the physical and spiritual worlds. From them, we may learn more about the realities of life from the spiritual perspective, and by translating that into our own lives, we begin to see our circumstances from a much larger point of view.

The real message behind the idea of free will, when we look at it from the evolutionary perspective of Spiritism, is about this conscious growth, a duty of the human spirit. It is about the choices, decisions, and deliberate efforts that propel a spirit toward its ultimate destiny of true happiness and relative perfection. I have told you that this destiny is inevitable. Through the action of divine laws and through the help we receive from benefactors in the spirit realm, we will all get there, sooner or later. However, Spiritism teaches us about taking charge of our destiny. What this means is that it is up to each of us, through the choices that we make, to determine how long it will take us to progress through each evolutionary stage.

When we talk about our *inner voice*, this is actually our conscience, which serves as a personal navigation system. It guides us through life's travels, tells us the best way to go at each pass, and reroutes us when we get off track. This inner voice may also refer to the help and suggestions we receive from guardian spirits by way of intuition. None of us is ever left to make this journey without the offer of heavenly assistance. It is, however, up to us to lift our thoughts to heaven and thereby tune in to this source of inspiration and guidance.

Friends, this is only the tip of the iceberg, but if you find this discussion intriguing, if these ideas resonate with you or seem to be something worth looking into, and if you are ready to take charge of your destiny, I strongly encourage you to start exploring Spiritism.

12
A Blessing to Forget?

Logically speaking, reincarnation offers rational explanations for many aspects of life. Yet if we've lived before – that is, with different bodies, under different personas, in different periods throughout history, and maybe even in different worlds – why don't we remember those past lives? If our present experiences can serve to teach us about choices we made in past lives, how can we benefit from them if we don't have the slightest recollection of those decisions and actions? These are very common questions that people ask, and rightly so. At first glance, it only seems logical that we should remember those former incarnations. Fortunately, there are reasons why we typically don't. In fact, according to Spiritist teachings, this is actually a blessing.

First, let us be clear about the fact that we don't truly forget our past lives. Every detail is stored deep within our spirits' memories. This is one function of the perispirit. Discarnate spirits, for example, once reaching a certain stage of evolution, are often able to recall with greater ease at least some experiences that preceded their most recent incarnation. If needed, they can be helped to probe deeper into their memory bank, so as to bring up the memory of a particular incident or period in time. For those of us presently incarnated, however, we usually do not have any *conscious* memory of our past lives. It's important to point out that, at times, some of those recollections do surface, as in the documented cases of spontaneous past-life memories or through hypnosis–induced, past-life regressions. Still, these are only partial recollections of particular points in time, even if they do span over more than one lifetime. Also, they are still relatively rare.

Why can't we remember and how does this help us? One reason is that it may be a distraction. In today's day and age, we are constantly exposed to new information that almost seems to bombard us, coming at us from many different directions and sources. In the midst of this, we've experienced how the multitude of inputs can begin to divert our attention from the basic and most important things in our lives. Although the context is not exactly the same as past-life recollections, we are familiar with the feeling of information overload. This can give us a start at imagining what it might be like if we could remember one, several, or all of our past lives. Having such memories at the forefront of our awareness could make it difficult to focus on our present life.

At the very least, remembering so many details from our past may be distracting. However, the truth is that it could actually have an even stronger impact to the point of potentially interfering with our ability to fulfill the objectives set out for our present incarnation. To understand this, we need only consider that we often reincarnate among individuals with whom we share a goal of reconciling conflicts or disharmonies created in past life encounters. Such events from former lives may very well have involved a significant deal of hurt or pain on the part of one or both parties involved. They may even have roots that can be traced back through more than one incarnation. Consequently, it is quite natural for challenges to arise in the new relationships formed through these reencounters, manifesting as anything from minor frictions to severe aversions. The obstacles that result present opportunities for us to exercise charity and put into practice the knowledge we may have acquired through diverse sources of moral teachings. Such efforts are the means to overcoming resentment, pain, and guilt and replacing them with forgiveness, fraternity, and love.

Spiritual reunions intended to foster some sort of readjustment may not always reveal themselves so readily. Some simply offer possibilities for the cultivation of loving and mutually supportive relationships, which become healing balms capable of fully mending old wounds. Other encounters afford guilty spirits a chance to labor or sacrifice in benefit of those to whom they find themselves indebted as a result of yesterday's choices and actions. In reality, there are many different circumstances through which divine providence offers us the opportunity to make amends, bring peace to our hearts and minds, restore relationships, and open new pathways in our progressive march toward true happiness.

These reencounters are designed to help spirits meet the objectives of life in the material world. Picture such a reencounter involving you and one of your family members, a friend, or someone else who plays a significant role in your life. Consider what it would be like if one or both of you could remember all the details of whatever unfortunate events took place in the past. Don't we sometimes find it challenging to forgive hurtful behaviors, even relatively minor ones, when the related events took place within this lifetime? If we are not careful, we can carry resentment or allow those memories to resurface in light of new conflicts that arise somewhere down the road. Imagine remembering that this person in your life today was the transgressor who caused you a great deal of pain in a former incarnation. You may now be getting along well, cultivating new and lasting ties of solidarity in spite of the rocky road you once traveled. However, should yesterday's obstacles become fresh memories, they may interfere with today's hopeful path to harmony and love.

We can take the above scenario a step further. If your interactions with that individual in this life involve any significant tension, discord, or problems between you, then such a reality would likely be further aggravated by the clear awareness of past events. In turn, this could impair the possibility of sowing seeds of reconciliation. In either case, without requiring those past-life memories to be present at a conscious level, the circumstances that naturally arise in these relationships already afford opportunities for the exercise of tolerance, understanding, compassion, and cooperation. These efforts are the means by which wounded spiritual ties are healed.

We are not always the ones called to forgive past transgressors. Quite often, we are the ones looking for forgiveness. We seek relief from the pain of remorse triggered by the awareness of hurt that we caused to others. In such cases, it is making amends, repaying our debts, restoring harmony, and deserving forgiveness that become our personal objectives as we reincarnate together with one or more companions from a former lifetime. To this, we can add experiences that serve a similar purpose without necessarily involving individuals we knew in a past life. In either situation, the pain of remorse motivates a spirit to return to the material world, where one finds blessed opportunities for achieving reparation and healing. While the awareness of our former, misguided actions is always retained within our spiritual memory, this is often below the surface of conscious thought. It exerts a more subtle influence on the way we think and the circumstances to which we are drawn. Reincarnation, therefore, does not offer a complete escape from the workings of our conscience. It only places a sort of translucent veil of forgetfulness over what would otherwise be vivid, surface-level memories. In this way, reincarnation affords us the chance to face the obstacles and opportunities that life may present, without having the burden of painful and constant reminders of what we came to regret.

As you can see, this veil of forgetfulness is actually a manifestation of God's love. Still, you may question the merit earned through forgiveness and the restoration of harmony if this is done in the absence of past-life memories. Keep in mind that those goals are not reached without genuine effort on the part of those involved, and this is the key point. Divine justice does not do away with our responsibilities before eternal law or toward one another. Instead, through the compassion of our Creator, we are granted this blessing which simply empowers us to open doorways without taking away our responsibility to put one foot in front of the other and walk through them.

Once we acknowledge this process of spiritual evolution, new questions may surface. For example, we may ask: How can we measure the degree of progress we've made thus far? Can we identify what we should work on during this present incarnation? To answer these questions, we are encouraged to observe ourselves carefully and regularly so that we come to recognize our tendencies and inclinations. The more naturally a virtue comes to us, the greater the extent to which it represents a personal, spiritual acquisition earned through morally sound choices and behaviors over the course of many lifetimes. On the other hand, any negative traits, habits, or temptations regularly characterizing our thoughts and behaviors indicate imperfections that we have yet to overcome. They may also represent spiritual conflicts or disharmonies that we carry with us from our past. Meanwhile, we can often gain some insight into the events of our spiritual history by observing and reflecting on these tendencies in combination with the experiences and challenges we face in this lifetime. There is no definitive, magical formula for determining the details of our past. Nor is it necessary to have vivid recollections in order to take advantage of present opportunities. In fact, for reasons already mentioned, such memories can even be detrimental.

As you can see, the blessing of temporarily forgetting our past allows us to stay forward-looking. This gives us the chance to focus on today's progress and tomorrow's happiness, without the potentially debilitating impact of having to remember the woeful and dolorous events of yesterday. In this sense, Spiritist knowledge is a valuable resource, for it makes us aware of the significance of our relationships. Its teachings change our perspective with regard to what the circumstances of these human interactions mean for us as eternal spirits. They give us ample reason and motivation to approach our relationships with the desire to be compassionate and loving in our thoughts and actions. Spiritism demonstrates that, in this way, we will one day inherit the kingdom of heaven – not alone or in the absence of any single loved one, but with our entire, integrated and perfectly harmonious spiritual family built through the irreversible bonds of our collective progress.

13
Why Does God Allow Suffering?

I mentioned briefly, in a previous chapter, about the role that hardships and difficulties play when they serve as opportunities for us to make amends or learn valuable, needed lessons. I think it's important to address the concept of suffering in more detail. After all, pain and sorrow have in some way been present throughout history, and yet, in spite of the religions, philosophies, sciences, and other sources we turn to for explanation, many people ask why there is so much suffering in the world. Whether it is pain we experience in our own lives, tragedy or heartbreak we witness among those close to us, or devastation we find in the daily news, suffering is all around. It knows no cultural, racial, social, or geographic boundaries. In fact, even when we observe those who exhibit noble sentiments, living their life with upright conduct and serving as a source of happiness, comfort, and inspiration for others, we find that they too are not safe from the touch of pain. Ultimately, we may sit back and think, "If there's truly someone or something in charge, why do such bad things happen to good people?" or "If God, our Creator, is truly all-powerful and infinitely good, why do we see so much anguish around us?"

Furthermore, some may feel as if "salt gets thrown into the wound" when, upon feeling at their lowest or in mourning the seemingly unjustified agony that others are undergoing, along come these messages about the need to be positive. Such advice is often accompanied by the additional suggestion to believe that life is not about the things that happen to us, but how we react to them. For many, this guidance is only motivational if they have the vision, understanding, and faith to support it. Otherwise, it can be no easy pill to swallow for those who still long to comprehend why such things happen or why they happen to certain people and not to others. This is where Spiritism helps us by showing us not only that the painful things that happen *do* have meaning, but why, indeed, the way we handle them is also very important. Spiritism teaches us that our reactions don't merely affect how we experience those times of trial and anguish in the present; they also determine what future outcomes will result, either later in this life or down the road. Many misguided souls curse their struggles, thus missing out on opportunities to make the best of them, simply because they lack the vision to see them from a perspective not limited to a single lifetime. However, Spiritism shows us that suffering represents God's will for us to be free and experience complete happiness. It illustrates how our reactions to the various trials of life carry the potential for allowing our suffering to serve its noble purpose, which is to clear self-made shadows from our pathway and allow the sun to shine after the passing of the storm.

As I've already stated, suffering can be found in all places. This is true in both the material and spiritual worlds. As for the spiritual world, suffering is found among those who create such a reality for themselves. Since I have addressed that in the chapter devoted to the spiritual realm, I will focus here on suffering in the material world.

◊ ◊ ◊

When it comes to a philosophy that includes reincarnation, people frequently associate present suffering with past-life causes, and they often have in mind the concept of *karma*, a term which, in my perception, is often thrown about quite loosely by those unaware of its true meaning. Not uncommonly, this term is thought of with a negative, sometimes fatalistic connotation. However, the concept itself, referring to actions and their consequences, is neutral. Remember the lesson about how you can tell a tree by its fruit[37]? Well, just as the tree itself determines the quality of the fruit, the nature of one's actions will likewise impact the kind of consequences that result. This applies to what we experience today as a result of yesterday's actions, as well as what we will encounter tomorrow as a consequence of today's choices. In Spiritism, we talk about this as the *law of cause and effect*. Even the name of this law denotes an easier-to-grasp definition of what really happens. When we delve deeper into the Spiritist texts, we find that the process does not work like a mere boomerang coming back to hit us with whatever we "put out into the universe." Spiritism shows us that it is very personal and involves a logical sequence of events put into place. In addition, we see this not as a crude means of *getting what one deserves*, good or bad, but as the working of divine laws which ensure our gradual process of purification and our complete understanding of love.

    I will not begin to discuss cause and effect by starting with past-life causes of suffering. We must first keep in mind that we can't always point to our previous incarnations in an attempt to explain misfortunes of the present. In other words, we are perfectly capable of bringing suffering upon ourselves within the present life, just by the thoughts we entertain, the attitudes we have, and the choices we make. In fact, we're quite good at it, too. This is why the advice of ancient wisdom, to *know thyself*, whether attributed to Socrates or another source, is crucial to our ability to identify ways in which we cause ourselves to suffer. Then we may make efforts to avoid

---

[37] The New Testament: Matthew 7:17–18.

the same mistakes going forward. In doing so, we need to keep ourselves in check and be honest. Therefore, we may ask ourselves these questions: How are we treating others? Are we controlling our emotions and measuring our words in a concerted effort to do no harm? Are we taking the thoughts, feelings, and needs of others into consideration, or are we being selfish? Are we humble or prideful? Are we patient and kind or disrespectful and cruel? Are we understanding and forgiving, or are we judgmental and intolerant?

At the same time, it's not just about others. In fact, we can't truly love others if we don't first love ourselves. So we should also ask: Are we giving ourselves a fair chance to take advantage of opportunities that come into our path, or are we negatively talking our way out of them? Are we giving value to those who motivate, encourage, or love us as unconditionally as is humanly possible, or are we foolishly striving to please those who don't really support us? Are we living within our means and prioritizing what really matters in life, or are we creating false needs and giving too much value to material things? Are we staying focused on important objectives, or are we wasting time and energy by "sweating the small stuff"? Are we being humble and forgiving ourselves for our mistakes, or do we repeatedly beat ourselves up for failures? Are we eating healthy and taking care of the body, or are we engaging in activities detrimental to our health? Are we being honest, expressing gratitude, cultivating positive thoughts, and trying to be good, or are we giving in to negative thoughts and inclinations?

The point is that we're still quite imperfect. If that weren't the case, this would be the last incarnation for all of us, and our ways would be quite different. The fact is that we're still learning. As such, we still make mistakes along the way, and we still complicate things for ourselves. By the law of cause and effect, these situations become the potential causes of less-than-pleasant present or future effects. I say potential because God is always just, and in some cases, our virtuous actions earn us merits that can help to mitigate such consequences.

Within the context of reincarnation, another important point is that in our perispirit, we carry the records of all our past thoughts and actions, including not only the advancements we've made but also our errors and mistakes. In this life, we often deal with inferior tendencies inherited as remnants of negative behaviors in past lives, behaviors that we've not yet eliminated from our personal conduct. We can also carry in our unconscious memory unresolved remorse for our past mistakes. Aside from the very details of the obstacles and difficulties we encounter, these additional conditions provide further explanation for why it can be difficult to do what we know is right or best. They also represent one reason why we come back to the material life. We need to work on each of them until we can claim full victory by liberating our conscience, overcoming weaknesses, and developing virtues to take their place.

In Spiritism, we have several resources to help us in this process of fighting inferior tendencies and cultivating virtuous ones. These resources do not merely point out areas for improvement. They also help us to see people and events from a different and more compassionate angle, which then inspires us to make worthwhile changes. Two of the most important and fundamental resources are Kardec's *The Gospel According to Spiritism* and *The Spirits' Book*. I like to say that *The Spirits' Book* helps us get our mental house in order with clarifications that set things straight and answer our most pertinent questions, thus allowing us to move on with hearts and minds open to the priceless moral wisdom contained within *The Gospel According to Spiritism*. There are other books, as well, through which the loving message of the noble and enlightened spirits shines; they, too, help us navigate through life, steer clear of obstacles, and head in the right direction. Incidentally, it's always advisable to go back and re-read from *The Spirits' Book* and *The Gospel According to Spiritism* because the more life experiences we have and the more we learn from further studies, the more we appreciate different aspects of the treasures contained in both.

◊ ◊ ◊

Having made the point that suffering doesn't always find its cause in a past life, we can now talk about situations where it does. First, however, a couple of preemptive statements are in order. So many are the forms of suffering that we cannot talk about each situation one could experience, and I will actually refrain from discussing any specific circumstances; innumerable examples, however, can be found in other Spiritist resources. Likewise, we must be careful not to draw black and white lines that trace a particular form of suffering to any definitive cause. We must be equally as careful with specific cases that are absent of pertinent details from a trustworthy source. This is because each case is in some way unique. Fortunately, God and our spiritual benefactors always take into account the degree of knowledge of those involved, as well as the full circumstances behind any action.

Though the degree to which we experience them will vary, difficulty, hardship, disappointment, loss, and the like are a part of life in this world. Generally speaking, when they result from events of a former incarnation, we can say that we are somehow reaping the consequences of what we sowed in the past. It is worth noting, so as to avoid confusion with any previously held conceptions, that we only harvest the results of what we, ourselves, have planted. Likewise, only we can correct our own wrongs. The lessons are ours to learn, and we are held fully accountable for our own actions. This includes our behaviors that are in any way responsible for provoking the actions of others. In accordance with divine justice, we will then acquire the debt or the reward thereby merited.

As I've mentioned previously, our lives are governed by a set of moral laws. These laws determine which behaviors will bring about happiness and which will lead to suffering. The behaviors that result in suffering are ones that mark our souls with imperfections and add liabilities to our evolutionary balance of moral merits and debts. This balance is something we carry with us as we progress from one incarnation to the next. Our merits are ours to keep forever, whereas our debts are temporary and last only until the imperfections are erased, thus freeing our conscience. Reincarnation is the missing puzzle piece needed to explain how that happens. It is a blessing from God, for the door is always open for us to return and make amends for our mistakes, to value what we once failed to appreciate, and to continue on the pathway of good, no matter how far we ever deviate from it. Regardless of how frequently we stumble or how badly we fall, we will always rise and march forward with the help of a God who never abandons a single one of his children.

Within Spiritist literature, there are many valuable descriptions of this process made possible by reincarnation. These include allegories and visualizations that help clarify the process and steer us away from understanding it as punishment when, in fact, it is a blessing. For example, through Kardec's writings, we learn to see the material world as a school or hospital where these painful experiences and the lessons we take from them help us to learn, grow, and heal; we also encounter individuals who, not unlike teachers, nurses, and doctors, help us to endure these experiences. In one example from the book *Heaven and Hell*, Kardec writes, "Spirits who are being punished are not like galley slaves sentenced to years of hard labor, but rather are like patients in a hospital who are suffering from an illness because of their own fault and who must now endure the required means of cure with the hope of finally being healed".[38] In his book *Life and Destiny*, Léon Denis, offers another type of imagery.[39] He compares a soul in transformation to a piece of raw material to be sculpted, whereby the hammering, chiseling, and molding, in representing either the blows of our suffering or the efforts that we make to effectuate our own progress, all serve to shape the soul's character and reveal its beauty. Furthermore, he adds that when the sculptor himself becomes mired in this process, sorrow comes along and helps, not only by keeping the work going but by doing so with the persistence and precision necessary to eliminate the rough edges that would otherwise stand in the way of revealing the beautiful shape in formation.

Sometimes we learn through our suffering or become shaped by it when it affords us opportunities to understand the error of our past ways. We can take the aforementioned analogy of sculpture from Léon Denis to help illustrate. For

---

[38] See item 30 in Chapter VII of *Heaven and Hell* by Allan Kardec [original title in French: *Le Ciel Et L'Enfer*, published in 1865], translation © 2006 by the International Spiritist Council, published in 2008 by the International Spiritist Council.

[39] See Chapters: "Sorrow" and "The Revelation of Sorrow", in *Life and Destiny* by Léon Denis [original title in French: *Le Problème de l'être et de la Destinée*, published in 1889], translation to English by Ella Wheeler Wilcox [published by London Gay & Hancock Ltd. in 1919], as prepared and made available online in electronic version by the Spiritist Alliance for Books.

example, we may learn by experiencing humiliation under the hammer of someone else's pitiful pride and cruelty to value the importance of humility and respect for others. We may learn by suffering privation under the chisel of someone else's selfishness and greed to value compassion, generosity, and solidarity. Through the blow of an incarnation cut short, our spirits may learn to value the gift and blessing of life itself.

Interestingly, experiences that afford opportunities for readjustment don't always come in forms that one might imagine. An enlightening example can be found in comments made by the spirit Joanna de Ângelis[40] in the book *After the Storm,* psychographed by the medium, Divaldo Franco[41]. Joanna points to individuals whose irresponsibility and

---

[40] Joanna de Ângelis "is highly accomplished and experienced in educational and evangelical work. Throughout several incarnations, she has been dedicated to the work of Jesus. Her last incarnation was in the city of Salvador (1761-1822) as Sister Joana Angélica de Jesus; in that lifetime, she became a martyr of the Brazilian Independence. In her previous incarnation, she lived in Mexico (1651-1695) as Sister Juana Inés de la Cruz, who became known as the greatest poetess of the Hispanic language. She also lived at the time of St. Francis of Assisi (sec. XIII), as she presented herself to the medium Divaldo Franco, in Assisi." In addition, "she lived in the first century as Joanna de Cusa, the merciful woman mentioned in the Gospel; she was buried alive beside her son and other Christians in the Coliseum of Rome. Through Divaldo Franco's psychographic work, Joanna de Ângelis is the spirit channeled in 58 works." (details found on book flap of *Family Constellation* by Joanna de Ângelis- English translation © 2010 by Centro Espírita Caminho da Redenção, published by Livraría Espírita Alvorada Editora [original title in Portuguese: Constelação Familiar, © 2008]).

[41] Divaldo Pereira Franco is one of the most well-known, contemporary mediums and speakers among those who work in the study, practice and dissemination of Spiritism as codified by Allan Kardec. He is also a distinguished humanitarian whose works have made a difference in the lives of a great number of individuals. With the guidance of his spiritual mentor, Joanna de Ângelis, Divaldo has psychographed over 200 books, including numerous books by Joanna, as well as many by several other spiritual authors. In 1952, Divaldo co-founded a charitable institution known as Mansion of the Way in the Brazilian state of Bahia; it provides daily housing, care, and education to orphaned children, including more than 3,000 children and teenagers. You can read more about Divaldo Franco and this institution at the websites DivaldoFranco.net and MansionOfTheWay.com.

neglect in a prior life were instrumental in major tragedies. As part of her discussion on the Spiritist view regarding disasters, Joanna explains that in a subsequent incarnation, such souls may encounter the opportunity to give their own life in a service of rescue. She says that by returning "to the same stage where they had transgressed," they "now become heroes by saving others at the cost of their own sacrifice, thus earning their peace." [42] From a perspective limited to this singular lifetime, we can see the bravery and nobility of these individuals who make such a sacrifice, but we would tend to view the outcome as only a tragedy. The broader perspective afforded by Joanna's explanation illustrates the degree of organization in God's design, where we find that everything has a reason and that God makes no mistakes.

In the same book I mentioned before, Léon Denis offers additional insight into pain, sorrow, and the various roles they play in aiding our spiritual progress. For example, he talks about how sorrow helps us to "see and feel a thousand delicate and powerful things". If you pay attention, you'll notice how suffering helps open our vision to new perspectives. At times, it gives us pause to stop and smell the roses when we'd otherwise not even notice them in our path. Other times, it may just stop us in our tracks and force us to take account of our lives, reevaluate things, and make needed changes. Even when we have no chance to make changes or take action, such as in the case of a prolonged illness toward the end of an incarnation, which we may ignorantly judge to be a cruel form of suffering, God knows what he is doing. In this case, the duration of the illness allows the spirit time to

---

[42] See Chapter 1 "Disasters" in *After the Storm* [original title in Portuguese, *Apos a Tempestade*] by Joanna de Ângelis and psychographed by the medium Divaldo Pereira Franco, © 1990 by Centro Espírita Caminho da Redenção in Bahia, Brazil, translation published by Livraría Espírita Alvorada Editora in Bahia, Brazil.

reflect, thus preparing the spirit to be received with due protection upon leaving the material world.

Denis also writes about the ability of suffering to "free imprisoned virtues". What could he mean by that? In one example, people who have lived through extremely difficult experiences often talk about discovering an inner strength they never knew they had. Perhaps you have experienced this yourself. Though digging deep and finding this strength may catch one by surprise, such discoveries also unlock a newfound sense of courage and self-confidence, and they teach us to push beyond the limits of what we think we can handle. Another example arises in those times when life puts us into very arduous circumstances for which the development or release of some particular virtue (or virtues) represents our only choice for enduring the situation without further aggravating our condition. The very challenges that our spirits withstand and overcome thus open doors and give flight to our sleeping virtues. Finally, suffering experienced first-hand makes us much more sensitive to the hardships of those around us. It is remarkable how often we find individuals who feel inspired by their own pain to either comfort, inspire, or protect others. In such cases, adversities awaken a sense of connectedness and reveal the virtue of compassion toward others who struggle.

◊ ◊ ◊

At our current stage of evolution, it is not uncommon for us to face problems and adversities that we've done nothing in the present life to cause. As mentioned, these are often the result of our poor choices in the past, and in such cases, they serve as a mechanism of education and equilibrium. However, in *The Gospel According to Spiritism*, where we find that very explanation, we also find Kardec's warning against categorically pointing to past wrongdoings as the source of any and all suffering not caused by actions taken in the present life. [43] This is because spirits will sometimes willingly choose to undergo a difficult trial simply to test themselves for a particular moral acquisition. If successful, they will earn an accelerated advancement of their progress. The experiences involved may be ones of readily apparent hardship or misfortune. However, this is not always the case. Sometimes, these trials do not overtly reveal such significance but do nonetheless entail a considerable moral accountability in addition to the potential for less obvious forms of suffering; this may be the case behind one's wealth, great beauty, exceptional talent, or fame.

There are yet other reasons why an incarnating spirit will willingly agree to face some particularly difficult circumstances. For example, the spirit may wish to help a loved one endure a painful trial. On other occasions, the spirit's goal may be to serve in some way as a positive example for others. Similarly, there are spirits who've already made significant moral progress but willingly reincarnate among the suffering, where they will labor anonymously in service to such communities. By demonstrating heroic self-denial and sacrifice in their fulfillment of such commitments, these souls acquire new degrees of spiritual purification. Consequently, they gain access to more advanced worlds in both the spiritual and material realms.

It is those spirits who endure their afflictions with the greatest resignation and faith, as well as the least amount of complaining or revolt, who will best take advantage of them to achieve their intended purpose. These reflections remind me of another passage from Léon Denis, in *Life and Destiny*,

---

[43] See Chapter V "Blessed Are the Afflicted".

where he reminds us that all the great men and women so highly esteemed throughout history have greatly suffered, not to mention the countless unsung heroes whose silent pain but relentless determination were witnessed by only a few. Wisely, he remarks, "Take away the sorrow, and you take away that which is most worthy of the admiration of the world, the courage which supports it!" [44] Later, he adds that these souls have taught us that "it is by duty and by suffering borne worthily that we blaze the trail to Heaven." What a powerful visual.

Courage in the face of suffering is also something echoed in the aforementioned chapter of *The Gospel According to Spiritism*. There we find explanations about the importance of making every effort we can to handle our problems with courage, resignation, patience, faith, and determination. If we give in to despair, we wind up clouding our vision, and we act out in ways we will later regret. We also create energies that impair our emotional and physical well-being, and we interrupt our mental connection with good spirits who are ready and willing to help us. At the same time, if we don't vigorously battle to overcome the darker vestiges of our past, we delay our progress by forgoing valuable opportunities for healing and renewal. Likewise, we can create the potential for even harder times down the road. So let's learn from this advice while we still have the chance. It's never too late to start.

◊ ◊ ◊

---

[44] See Chapter XXVI "Sorrow" in *Life and Destiny* by Léon Denis [original title in French: *Le Problème de l'être et de la Destinée*, published in 1889], translation to English by Ella Wheeler Wilcox [published by London Gay & Hancock Ltd. in 1919], as prepared and made available online in electronic version by the Spiritist Alliance for Books.

The spirits teach us that God knows what is best and does not give us more than we can handle. He also knows what we feel and how we suffer at all times. When we cry out in pain and tears, our lamentations do not go unheard. Let us reflect on how good parents, in wisdom and in love, set boundaries, establish limitations, and discipline their children while at times allowing them to learn from their own mistakes. God, who loves us more deeply than any parent on Earth has ever loved a child, does the same for us and more. Similarly, we know that doctors allow their patients to undergo painful treatments and procedures for the sake of their ultimate healing. Again, God, in his profound compassion, allows us to feel pain as a way to restore our spiritual well-being. Finally, wherever possible, whenever merited, and especially when we are open to receiving heavenly support, it will be there to help us through these temporary storms. We have friends in the spirit realm who are ready to come to our aid. Some can provide rather direct, albeit unseen, help. Others, who sympathize with our condition, or regard us with an affection established sometime in the past, pray fervently for God's intervention. They ask God to bless us with strength, resistance, perseverance, and peace.

Sometimes, people are surprised to learn that we often choose and even ask for our particular trials and expiations before beginning a new incarnation. However, this is precisely what happens since God's laws require us to take an active role in the course of our spiritual lives. There are other times when we are not in a condition to make such decisions. In such cases, our spiritual mentors will do so on our behalf. There is definitely truth in this popular expression: "Everything happens for a reason." The good thing is that, in light of the Spiritist teachings, those seemingly unfair situations that might have once led us to question God's ways now have an explanation. Through Spiritism, we have a better way to understand suffering, and our faith in God's wisdom and mercy is restored.

Ignorance of these laws and processes makes it more difficult to find justice in the suffering of the world or the courage to face our problems with hope and determination. However, with the knowledge and reason gained through the study of Spiritism, the picture becomes clearer. We know that God is looking after all of us, from those who stubbornly persist in wrongdoing, thus creating for themselves a painful future, to those who pass through this life dedicating themselves to the good and thereby earning merit for future rewards. Nonetheless, for each of us suffering is a part of our spiritual growth, and the divine laws apply equally to all. As such, in God's wisdom and mercy, the hardships of today become the blessings of tomorrow. Through the understanding of Spiritism, we will learn to transform our sorrows, as we find a solid foundation for faith and the whole-hearted belief that divine justice never fails.

14
Spiritual Mentors and Friends:
The Comfort of Knowing They're There

Inevitably, there are situations in life that find us facing uncertainties, fears, or difficult emotions. Having the support of friends and loved ones to help us through those rough times is truly a blessing. However, those individuals don't always have all the answers. At the same time, they can never fully know what we are feeling or thinking in our innermost thoughts. It's especially trying when we feel alone without anyone to turn to. Some moments like this are passing and, overall, not so bad. We may have a rough day or a difficult week. We may have a decision on which we're wavering, but the stakes are relatively low. Somehow, we work our way through it. At other times, in our darker hours, we may feel great sadness, anger, fear, or shame. We may feel overwhelmed with tears or want to scream and shout.

Picture yourself in one of those moments, whether it be a passing challenge or a time filled with great anguish. Now imagine right by your side a friend like no other. This loyal friend is always there when needed, never judges you, and always has your best interest in mind. This friend hears your cries for help and knows the indecisions that trouble you. In fact, aside from knowing what you are feeling inside, this friend often knows more about your situation than you do. This amazing, truly God-sent companion is your spirit guide, unseen in most cases but there nevertheless. In fact, we always have guides and mentors beside us in both realms of life. As for the material realm, each of us has a spirit in the discarnate state who previously accepted the calling to accompany and guide us through our journey in the material world. This is why a spirit guide may also be called a spiritual mentor. Think of this spirit as one who, just like you, is traveling the path of spiritual evolution but is simply at a point further down the road. Having some wisdom and experience with which to help you, the spirit guide will give you advice. He or she may also seek further support from others in the spiritual or material realm when this is both needed and deserved. Aside from having accompanied you since your birth, your guide is also aware of pertinent details from your past lives and has knowledge of your primary objectives for this incarnation. The next time you find yourself in need of guidance, strength, calm, or will, just picture your spirit guide there with you. Such thoughts work in the form of evocation. So go ahead. Call your spirit guide, and take comfort in the presence of this wonderful friend.

◊ ◊ ◊

Some may wonder if our personal spirit guides are the only ones able to help us. Absolutely not! Aside from them, we have around us other friendly, good-willed spirits whom we also refer to as spirit guides, mentors, benefactors, or friends. They truly look out for us. These may be spirits personally known to us or ones who simply have an affinity with us and become attracted to us by our thoughts and interests. They, too, can help us in many of the same ways that our personal, spiritual mentor can. Beyond the individual level, there are benevolent spirits who comfort, help, guide, and protect us at the level of families, communities, and other socially organized units – even nations and worlds. The order in creation is truly amazing, and the spiritual community – with its hierarchy based on moral and intellectual evolution, combined with its network of relationships – is very much a part of that. As you explore further into Spiritist literature, you will be amazed at how closely and frequently our two realms interact.[45]

One very important lesson from Spiritism is that our spiritual benefactors never impose upon our free will. The exercise of free will is one of the key mechanisms in our spiritual growth, and in obedience to God's will, good and elevated spirits will never cross this line. This means that they act in a more concealed way. They can help us receive good energies, assist by strengthening our will, offer advice, or encourage us to see things from new perspectives. However, they will never tell us exactly what to do, force us to take any particular action, or tell us that a particular event will surely happen. Ultimately, the decisions are ours as are the consequences that follow.

You may be wondering how you can receive this guidance if you don't see spirits, hear spirits, or channel them in any way. In reality, we all receive some level of influence from spirits. Just as we may sense the energy or detect the thought waves of other incarnate spirits, we can capture (more easily) the vibrations and thoughts of discarnate spirits, particularly those with whom we have an affinity. When we do not hear them directly, we register these thoughts at an unconscious level, and we perceive them by way of intuition. Sometimes we can recognize this happening when we almost literally feel a thought "pop into our heads." Most times, however, the action is much more subtle, and we do not recognize the idea as coming from an external source. This is OK. The important thing is that we have received the help.

---

[45] To read more about the help that we on Earth receive from spiritual benefactors, I would recommend Kardec's books, as well as the books *The Messengers* and *Between Heaven and Earth* by the spirit author André Luiz and the medium Francisco Cândido Xavier.

Our vision has been amplified. It is up to us to make good use of the advice. The more we know ourselves and the more vigilant we are, the better we can register instances of spiritual influence. Finally, while it's always important to give thanks in prayer for all the help we receive from the spiritual realm, it's also a wonderful idea to offer a simple thought of gratitude whenever we feel we have been inspired in a beneficial way.

Affinity and mental connection are keys to determining the kind of spiritual influence we receive. This is simply the law of attraction at work. Our own thoughts and energies literally tune us to those of like-minded spirits. Good spirits are never far from us. Depending on the ideas we nurture and the habits we cultivate, we either become closer to them and more receptive to their suggestions, or we distance ourselves from them and become less receptive to their influence.

When we choose to exercise kindness, respect, tolerance, compassion, honesty, humility, etc., we elevate our own vibrations. We do the same by practicing patience, resignation, self-control, integrity, sacrifice, and perseverance. Furthermore, our willingness and efforts to face our trials with resignation, determination, and faith also brighten the inner light that shines in our soul. These attitudes and behaviors help us to maintain beneficial connections with good spirits, and they make us deserving of their support.

This kind of intuitive suggestion is not the only way we receive guidance from spiritual mentors. I'll bet that more than once after going to sleep with some kind of trouble or question on your mind, you have awoken with a new perspective, maybe even an answer you were looking for. During our moments of sleep, while our physical bodies are at rest, our spirits become temporarily liberated from the physical body in such a way that we are free to travel to the places to which our thoughts and vibrations direct us. These include places in both the material and spiritual realms. [46] We roam through the environments that our spirits desire to be in, and we visit the individuals who our souls long to see. Therefore, it is not uncommon for us to seek the company of our spirit guides and friends. Upon awakening, we may not consciously remember most or any of these such encounters, but they do represent an opportunity for open dialogue with our spirit guides. Occasionally, when we have trouble making a decision or finding the solution to a problem, someone will say, "Sleep on it, and things will look better in the morning." This is one reason why that prediction can come true.

    Our spiritual mentors are there to help us. So don't be shy with them. Feel free to ask for help,[47] and be sure to give thanks for their assistance.

---

[46] While incarnate, our spirits are never fully separated from the physical body, which would result in the death of the latter. During these moments of partial liberation, they remain connected to the body through a semi material link, referred to as the silver cord (mentioned in Ecclesiastes 12:6), which has been reported to be seen by other discarnate spirits (as shared via mediumistic communication), as well as by some mediums communicating in a somnambulistic trance.

[47] See also Chapter 16 "Prayer".

15
Beware of Bad Company

The good news about the law of attraction is that it facilitates our connection with kind and loving spirits. On the other hand, this same natural law allows us to be influenced in a negative way should we open the door for such persuasion. We ultimately benefit from the resulting experiences that become a tool in our spiritual learning process. However, rather than learning lessons the hard way, our goal should be to avoid or resist negative influences as much as possible. Therefore, we have here a danger for which we must be on the lookout. At our stage of evolution, this harmful influence occurs more often than most of us could ever imagine. Fortunately, Spiritism equips us with valuable knowledge and important precautions we can take.

Since we are still learning about immortal and evolving spiritual life, God does not expect us to be perfect at this stage in our development. What matters is that we are always working on self-improvement. The more our thoughts and actions are inspired by compassion, and the more they are driven by conscious efforts to develop moral virtues, the higher will be the frequency of our spiritual energies. This helps us in multiple ways. First of all, these energies contribute to the health of our spiritual body and, by consequence, the well-being of our physical body. Second, they attract the company of good spirits. Lastly, these energies help us form a protective barrier against the unfavorable impact of ignorant, frivolous, or ill-meaning spirits, whether their influence is intentional or not.

Spirits influence one another whether they are incarnate or discarnate. In this chapter, I will focus specifically on how discarnate spirits can negatively influence those living in the material world. Even without detailed discussion on all the ways this can happen, a few examples will illustrate how our mental and emotional states predispose us to such interactions. In some cases, the influence is not targeted or personal. It may merely be a case of mutual attraction. In other cases, the discarnate spirit may wish to satisfy some kind of artificial need[48]. As the familiar saying goes, misery loves company. We could actually substitute any descriptive state for the word *misery* in the sense that "like attracts like". Therefore, spirits who persistently nurture negative thoughts and feelings find company in those of us who do the same.

In a somewhat more intentional yet still non-personal manner, a spirit might also provoke the persistence, or aggravation, of our negative emotions or attitudes. They may do this simply for the enjoyment of witnessing the unfortunate actions they can incite within us. Other times, the disturbed spirit may be one who in his or her last material life suffered without rectification from an addiction. This could have taken the form of substance abuse, sexual promiscuity or addiction, materialistic infatuation, or some other unhealthy behavior. In returning to the discarnate state, the spirit's mental fixation on the satisfaction attained through such behaviors remains active. The spirit, therefore, continues to seek such gratification. Upon finding incarnate souls who take part in the same lamentable activities, the suffering spirit will seek vicarious enjoyment by feeding off the energies created by those who engage in such behaviors.

---

[48] Suffering spirits sometimes indirectly nurture their inferior appetites by relishing the energies that we create as we engage in the unhealthy behaviors that those spirits enjoyed when last living in the material world.

Aside from the above situations, there are many cases in which the negative influence is both intentional and personal. When this happens, the ill-willed spirit acts with an agenda, usually driven by feelings of spite, resentment, vengeance, or the like. We may be the direct object of this attention or a mere pawn in the spirit's ultimate objective of targeting a third party. Such circumstances may be short-lived or long-lasting depending on the objectives and determination of such a spirit, as well as the degree to which we open ourselves up to this kind of influence. When the negative influence is persistent, Spiritism refers to this disturbance as a *spiritual obsession*. This is a process that can take place in varying degrees and forms. In any case, Spiritism makes us aware of this danger and offers guidance on how to protect ourselves from it. In addition, the truly Spiritist way is always one of love and compassion, which is reflected in the Spiritist approach to understanding and responding to cases of spiritual disturbance.

Just as the angelic or morally advanced spirits are not beings apart from creation, neither are the ones still learning who continue to make very unfortunate choices. Any spirit, incarnate or discarnate, who acts in the absence of love ultimately brings hurt to itself and others. The harsher and more damaging the actions are, the less naturally inclined we feel to view them with understanding. However, from the compassionate perspective of Spiritist teachings, we learn that at some level, such behaviors are driven by personal suffering and pain. God and the more advanced spirits know this, and they always see us from this standpoint. Meanwhile, at our present level of imperfection and in our limited view of the circumstances involved, it is natural for nearly all of us to feel disturbed, shocked, sometimes horrified to see unimaginable behaviors in our fellow human beings. Perhaps even more disturbing is to imagine them coming from invisible brothers and sisters in the spirit realm. Yet, the more we study Spiritism, the more we are able to grasp these concepts and look at a situation from the vantage point of Spiritist knowledge. Likewise, the greater is our propensity to forgive. We can even sympathize with the offenders, knowing the kind of debts they are acquiring, as well as the suffering they are susceptible to undergo as a result.

The Spiritist vision actually goes a step further. Spiritism teaches that if we are the object of a negative spiritual influence, we must not assume ourselves to be innocent victims. After all, how do we know just what our true involvement is in the story *behind* today's circumstances? Spiritism illuminates our understanding of how unresolved past-life events often spill over into the present; the corresponding circumstances often resemble the unfolding drama of a TV soap opera. Many times, today's perpetrators are yesterday's victims and vice-versa. In severe cases, these battles can go on for centuries with chapters that play out over multiple lifetimes. Fortunately, natural law, divine justice, and the compassion of our Creator all ensure that we will eventually bring this cycle of tragedy to an end. New chapters will take those age-old stories in a fresh direction, one of reconciliation and redemption.

Let us be clear that the influence of inferior, spiritual company does not require an obsession to be present. Quite frequently, the influence we undergo is only momentary. Consider how often we lose our temper or our patience, pass judgment, become unjustifiably upset over a disappointment, or fail to tolerate or forgive. These are the sign-posts that attract undesirable company. Meanwhile, every day we are exposed to environments where spirits of diverse categories may be present. To the same degree, we all face temptations toward disharmonized ideas and emotions. Hopefully we are keeping our momentary weaknesses of thought under control. Hence the need to be vigilant and the importance of making efforts to keep our thoughts well focused. When our imbalances persist without proper control, then the obsessions in their varying degrees and forms can develop.

At Spiritist Centers, the approaches for treating discovered cases of obsession are multifaceted. For certain, help is provided to the incarnate individual undergoing this process. This includes different forms of supportive energy healing. Likewise, both this individual and the members of his or her family or household are educated on their role in the healing process. They are encouraged to participate in morally uplifting studies both at home and at the Spiritist Center. They are also advised to be mindful and in control of their thoughts and behaviors. Meanwhile, the discarnate spirit is also helped, through counseling and treatments. The latter are made possible through special mediumship sessions where incarnate workers of the Spiritist Center join forces with collaborators and mentors from the spiritual realm. This service represents one example of the compassionate and noble use of mediumship according to the Spiritist vision and practice.

In the end, the knowledge we acquire from Spiritism illustrates why it is important to be so careful with what we think and how we act. These factors determine the kind of spiritual company and influences that we attract and to which we become receptive. They also help demonstrate why Jesus told us to forgive our enemies. Life, my friends, is indeed a school with many lessons on the grand subject of love.

16
Prayer

What is prayer? Why should we pray? Most certainly, *prayer* means different things to different people. In Spiritism, prayer is seen as an invaluable source of spiritual nourishment. Through my previous discussion on support from spiritual benefactors, I hinted at one form of prayer, meaning the turning of our thoughts to Heaven in request for help. I would like to expand on that to provide more details about the Spiritist perspective on the concept and practice of prayer.

First of all, not unlike other belief systems or even practices that come naturally to many people, we find in Spiritism mention of three general elements of prayer: asking for help, expressing appreciation, and giving praise. In some ways, taking time to express gratitude in prayer has a similar effect to writing down our blessings in a gratitude journal. This is not done for God's benefit but for our own. It gives us the opportunity to consciously reflect on blessings we have received. Gratitude is an exercise that becomes easier and more beneficial the more we practice it. As you may have noticed, it seems to have an almost automatic feedback loop that becomes increasingly powerful once we get it started.

In spite of that powerful momentum, the reality is that life presents us with many distractions. The various events of our day-to-day lives clamor for our attention, as do the myriad of thoughts continuously running through our minds. Because of this, it takes some effort to keep up with the practice of gratitude. However, those who have done so can attest that once you are in that mindset, you begin to appreciate things you might never have noticed before. In this way, we gain a greater vision of how fortunate we truly are. At the same time, by studying the divine laws, we come to understand how our experiences offer opportunities for learning, growth, reparation, and healing. Knowledge of that kind adds to our grateful mindset by giving us an appreciation for life's blessings in disguise.

Gratitude is also a way to keep our thoughts elevated, with balance and a positive focus. In doing so, we circulate healthy and renovating energies throughout our perispirit, whereby the resulting physical benefits may then transfer to the material body. Elevated thoughts are good for us in yet another way; they attract the company of those good-willed spirits who help us in so many ways. Our minds work similar to radios. They tune to the preferred frequencies at which we set them. The better the moral tuning of our minds and the greater the quality of our thoughts, the more positive are the outcomes we attract into our lives.

Here's a final piece of food for thought regarding prayers of appreciation. Do you recognize any people in your life who only call or write when they need something? For whatever reason, we sometimes act in exactly the same way toward God and our spiritual friends. With the busy nature of our daily activities and all that competes for our attention, it can easily become our habit to think of Heaven only when we find ourselves in need of help. Yet, giving thanks is such an important part of healthy living that we should be incorporating it into our daily lives and our prayers.

Praise, or reverence, in prayer works similarly to gratitude in that it helps to direct our thoughts and open our hearts and minds to a stronger connection with God and our spiritual benefactors. Expressing our acknowledgement of God's greatness is not done to satisfy some need God has, but rather to remind ourselves of God's goodness. When we deviate from humility, we begin to question God's will or wish to make suggestions. We sometimes make demands of our own as if we were wiser or knew better than God's divine laws. Therefore, including a simple expression of reverence, which does not have to be anything formal, puts us in a more humble mindset whereby we recognize God's position as our loving Father. We acknowledge our role as growing children who benefit from appreciating God's wisdom, mercy, support, and compassion. A deeper study of Spiritism also strengthens our understanding of this relationship with God.

Finally, there are times in prayer when we ask for help, either for ourselves or for others. Spiritism teaches that rather than requesting specific outcomes, we should primarily ask for things like courage, strength, resignation, patience, resistance to temptation, guidance, and clarity of thought. In our process of spiritual development, we are often like children, not knowing what our spirits truly need. We ask for things that may only satisfy our immediate human desires. We are unable to see the bigger picture which we only discover as we grow. Therefore, we need to place greater trust in God's will.

Inevitably, the next question from some will be, "If God and our spiritual mentors know what is best, why do we need to pray for help?" One reason is that if we ask as recommended above, prayer is an excellent way to express our desire for that kind of moral support. This ultimately opens us to receiving the requested assistance, and it helps us to endure our trials in such a way that we earn merit for a better future.

Prayer is also a great resource for helping someone else. When we pray for others, we send them positive vibrations, or good energies. Even if only at an unconscious level, they can receive those thoughts and energies and benefit from them. Likewise, the energies and thought forms that we create through this type of prayer are often used by higher order spirits who can assist in many interesting ways. This is such an easy way to practice charity. We should make it a regular practice to pray for those in need, including our loved ones, as well as complete strangers.

Let us remember that we can also include discarnate souls in our prayers. For example, those for whom we feel affection are likewise pleased to know that we remember them, and they can benefit from the good thoughts we send their way. Meanwhile, there are also discarnate strangers who find themselves in a variety of uncomfortable situations. These souls need loving vibrations from those willing to remember them in prayerful petitions.

It is always a good idea to pray for our enemies, as Jesus taught, even when they are unknown to us. Doing so is not only a form of charity and a meritorious exercise of love; it also helps us to keep rancor from our hearts, send good energies and spiritual aid to those whom we have offended, and protect ourselves from injurious vibrations. Finally, we can also pray for the continued strength of those who serve God by working selflessly for the good of others.

◊ ◊ ◊

Spiritism teaches that an effective prayer is one that comes from the heart. Our prayers gain travel power through intensity and sincerity. Humble intentions are also important. Truly, there is no need to scramble for fancy words or follow any formulas. In fact, these things may actually distract us from concentration and thoughtful expression. Humble and sincere thoughts are what connect us to God and our spiritual benefactors. All you must do is find a quiet time and place. Then simply open your heart, and share what's on your mind.

If you are not in the habit of praying, you might think it's hard to get started. Just think of it, however, like turning on an old rusty faucet, in which case it may take a little elbow grease to open the spigot for a steady stream of water. Prayer works in much the same way! Once you make a little effort to get started and establish the resulting connection, you'll be surprised at how the ideas start to flow. Soon, you'll make prayer a part of your daily life.

17
Jesus

Why do Spiritists emphasize Jesus and call themselves Christians? Who is Jesus in the Spiritist perspective? Doesn't Spiritism claim to bless any religious or spiritual beliefs capable of touching hearts, inspiring an empowering faith, and awakening the noblest of sentiments and actions? Perhaps you've asked yourself one or more of these questions. If that's the case, you are not alone. So let's take a closer look at what Spiritism tells us about Jesus because it is very important to clarify the answers to these commonly asked questions.

The first mention of Jesus in Spiritism occurred when the superior spirits answered this question from Kardec: "What is the perfect standard that God has offered to humankind as a guide and model?"[49] They replied, "Look at Jesus." As you will discover in Spiritist literature, we study Jesus' life and teachings. We follow him as our ultimate moral model and guide, and we believe that he is indeed "the way, the truth, and the life"[50]. We believe it is by following his lessons and examples that we will come to experience spiritual plenitude, true happiness, and the complete knowledge of our heavenly Father. Jesus' life on Earth was one of utmost humility, sacrifice, and love. Proving his absolute knowledge and assimilation of divine law, Jesus' words and actions soundly reflected his sincere faith and devotion to God.

---

[49] See question # 625 of *The Spirits' Book* by Allan Kardec [original title in French: *Le Livre des Espirits*, published in 1857 with 2nd edition in 1860], translation © 2006 by the International Spiritist Council, authorized edition printed in 2010 by Edicei of America.

[50] The New Testament: John 14:6.

This vision of Jesus comes to life in a whole new way when seen from the Spiritist view. We gain a new perspective on the significance of Jesus' time spent on Earth and the unique role he plays in relation to our world. We also acquire valuable insight about the meaning behind his numerous lessons.

A truly comprehensive discussion on the Spiritist view of Jesus would involve a much lengthier, if not voluminous reading. Spiritist books abound with narrations, reflections, and, in some cases, revelations that speak to both our hearts and minds, adding layer upon layer to our knowledge about Jesus. Truthfully, only a deeper study can offer such reward. Nonetheless, it is still of great importance that we take a look at this indispensable cornerstone of Spiritist studies and beliefs.

Who is Jesus?

Jesus said, "I and my Father are one" [51]. According to Spiritism, this statement refers to the harmonic alignment between the moral character of our brother Jesus and the essential nature of our shared Creator. In the Spiritist belief, Jesus, not unlike you and me, is a son of God. His spirit was created in the same way as all others, subject to the same natural laws, including the law of progress. Along his own evolutionary journey, Jesus advanced through the many stages of spiritual development and acquired ever progressive degrees of moral and intellectual advancement. In this way, he attained a state of perfect communion with our divine Creator and joined the ranks of pure spirits, who represent the highest category on the scale of spiritual evolution.

---

[51] The New Testament: John 10:30.

As Allan Kardec wrote in *The Spirits' Book*, spirits who belong to such a category "have ascended through all of the degrees of the hierarchy and have freed themselves from all the impurities of matter", whereby their role as pure spirits is to act as "the messengers of God, whose orders they carry out to maintain universal harmony." Kardec further explains that "they direct all the spirits beneath them, help them to perfect themselves and assign them their missions. They assist humans in their distress and inspire them to do good or to expiate the wrongs that keep them from supreme bliss." [52] Having reached this stage of evolution, Jesus' thoughts and actions are an untainted expression of the divine will. He, himself, is not God, but he is able to represent God in caring for those of us on Earth.

Jesus was called by God to be a caretaker of our planet, yet his role is even greater. He has been, in fact, the ultimate steward of the Earth since the start of its formation. In the book *On the Way to the Light*, written by the spirit author Emmanuel[53] and psychographed by the medium Francisco Cândido Xavier, Emmanuel elaborates on the information provided at the time of the Spiritist Codification, describing Jesus as the spiritual governor of the Earth, a

---

[52] See item 113 in Part Two, Chapter 1 of *The Spirits' Book* by Allan Kardec [original title in French: *Le Livre des Espirits*, published in 1857 with 2nd edition in 1860], translation © 2006 by the International Spiritist Council, authorized edition printed in 2010 by Edicei of America.

[53] Emmanuel was the spirit guide of the medium Francisco Cândido Xavier. He was the coordinator of Xavier's psychographic writing and personally authored 23 books of his own through Xavier's mediumship. Emmanuel's former incarnations include the Roman senator Publius Lentulus, who lived at the time of Jesus; the slave Nestorius; Father Manuel da Nobrega; and Father Damiano. Each of these personalities is the subject of a literary work authored by Emmanuel. Emmanuel's activity "is highlighted in the realms of study, practice, and dissemination of the Gospel of Jesus, under the light of the Spiritist Doctrine." (details on Emmanuel as found on the book flap to the novel *Paul and Stephen* by Emmanuel [original title in Portuguese: Paulo e Estevão], published in 2008 by the International Spiritist Council).

position commonly attributed to Jesus within Spiritist literature. Emmanuel writes:

"The traditions of the spirit world say that in the governance of all the phenomena of our system, there is a Community of Pure spirits, chosen by the Supreme Lord of the Universe, whose hands hold the guiding reins of all the life of all planetary collectivities.

From what we have been told, this Community – made up of perfected, angelic beings, of which Jesus is one of the divine members – has met in the vicinity of the Earth only twice, in the course of the known millennia, to decide on urgent issues pertaining to the organization and direction of our planet.

The first meeting took place when the terrestrial orb detached from the solar nebula, so that the demarcations of our cosmogonic system and the prototypes of life in the fiery matter of the planet could be set in space and time. The second occurred when the Lord's coming to the earth was determined in order to bring the immortal lesson of his Gospel of love and redemption to the human family." [54]

In this same book, Emmanuel goes on to describe various phases of the formation and pre-human, physical evolution of the planet Earth as directed by spiritual agents who worked under Jesus' careful administration. Following this discussion, he concentrates the greater part of his book on the history of civilization from the perspective of higher order

---

[54] See section "The Community of Pure Spirits" in Chapter 1 of *On The Way to the Light* [original title in Portuguese: *A Caminho da Luz*], translation © 2011 by the Brazilian Spiritist Federation, published in 2011 by the International Spiritist Council.

spirits in the spiritual realm. In this fascinating account, Emmanuel takes us through the formation and activity of some of history's most significant cultures, civilizations, and religions, synthesizing mankind's march through spiritual progress, so as to illustrate the wise and beneficent hand of Jesus, together with his honorable collaborators, throughout every era of Earth's historical trajectory.

Throughout this discussion, Emmanuel sheds light on the role of many individuals who, over the length and breadth of human history, have lived among us on Earth, sharing wisdom and knowledge about spiritual matters and divine natural laws. Indeed, the essence of Jesus' message[55] is found among the teachings of many estimable historical figures, thus having formed the basis of various religions and philosophies of this world. The heavens work hard to ensure that God's truths be known. Therefore, as many will point out, Jesus was not the first, nor the last, to elucidate to God's children the lessons of faith, love, and moral virtue. Spiritism teaches that the noble spirits who have dedicated themselves to such a cause have acted as emissaries of Christ; they have brought his message to the Earth in many ways to plant the appropriate seeds within the diverse populations that have existed since civilization first began.

Since the ground on which these seeds have been planted has not been completely fertile and nurturing,

---

[55] In the simplest expression, faith and love were the quintessential principles of Jesus' message, the essence of which is our relationship to God and to one another. His two greatest commandments were "'Love the Lord your God with all your heart and with all your soul and with all your mind" and, secondly, "Love your neighbor as yourself." (Matthew 22:36-40). Jesus taught about our brotherhood as children of one Creator and explained the merciful, just, and loving nature of our common Father. He instructed us to learn how to coexist in harmony, peace, and love, emphasizing this duty to love one another as the means by which we will one day achieve everlasting peace in the Kingdom of Heaven.

mankind has always found a way of distorting their rudimentary elements. The author Léon Denis, in his book *Here and Hereafter*, provides excellent imagery to illustrate how this can happen. He explains that like a dew drop that glistens with purity until it touches the ground and becomes "mingled with all the impurities thereof", the lessons of Jesus and others who've preached the "omnipresent and ever consistent" moral law have always become tainted. With time, they've undergone successive alterations, become grossly misinterpreted, and wound up "buried and forgotten beneath the rubbish of overlying symbolism."[56] Because of this, we have continued to receive moral reinforcements of all shapes and colors reflecting the spiritual realm's persistence in promoting the evolution of human souls.

As he brings the aforementioned book to a close, Emmanuel speaks as an advocate for our continued advancement, proclaiming the importance of the gospel of Jesus as clarified and illuminated by Spiritist teachings. These teachings have uncovered grand spiritual truths beneath layers of erroneous interpretations and misrepresentations developed over time. Emmanuel asserts that only Spiritism, "in its characteristic of renewed Christianity, can save the religions that are vanishing amid the collisions of power and ambition, of selfishness and domination, and point humankind toward its true path." So eloquently he writes, "In Spiritism's wellspring of enlightenment, humankind will be able to drink the crystalline water of the consoling truths of Heaven, enabling souls to prepare for a new age."

---

[56] See Chapter 1 of *Here and Hereafter* by Léon Denis [original title in French: *Aprés La Mort*, published in 1889], translation to English by George G. Fleurot in 1909, as printed in 2005 by the Spiritist Alliance for Books.

Jesus' Life on Earth

Understanding Jesus as a pure spirit and the governor or supreme steward of our planet gives us a whole new perspective on his incarnation in this world. We likewise discover a newfound appreciation for the sacrifice he made in this ultimate act of love. In Spiritist literature, we come to understand the descent that he made – leaving the blissful, celestial realms of the spiritual plane in order to be born into our rugged, material world, immersed in all the dense vibrations that characterized and to some degree do still characterize our planet's evolutionary stage. Prior to having the Spiritist knowledge, we were already aware of the cruel and relentless persecutions Jesus had to face. Driven by individuals who saw Jesus' influence as a threat to their power and dominion, these persecutions culminated in the great savagery that was his death on the cross. Amid the backward and violent ways that still dominated sectors of human behavior at that time, this loving and gracious shepherd was willing to come down and live among his lost sheep so that he could gather them and show them the way home. Again, in *On the Way to the Light*, Emmanuel describes the meeting between Christ and the "assemblies of his emissaries", saying that "it was then that the solar system's angelic spirits, in the proximities of the Earth, adopted measures of vast and magnificent importance. It was time for the teachings of the Savior to shine on human beings, controlling their freedom with the perfect exemplification of love." [57]

---

[57] See section "On the Eve of the Lord" in Chapter 11 of *On The Way to the Light* [original title in Portuguese: *A Caminho da Luz*], translation © 2011 by the Brazilian Spiritist Federation, published in 2011 by the International Spiritist Council.

In the first chapter of *The Gospel According to Spiritism*, Kardec highlights the purpose of Jesus' life on Earth by saying that it was to "fulfill the prophecies that foretold his coming". Kardec explains that Jesus came to develop the law defined in the Ten Commandments revealed by Moses, that is, "to give it meaning and to adapt it to the degree of humankind's advancement". Kardec points to Jesus' emphasis on the importance of duty to God and to one's neighbor and says that this teaching "comprises the basis of Jesus' doctrine." This duty is what Jesus and his collaborators saw lacking in the hearts and minds of men and women on Earth. Therefore, as Kardec also writes, Jesus came to "teach humans that true life is to be found not on Earth, but in the kingdom of heaven". He came to show them "the way that leads there", to demonstrate "the means of reconciling themselves with God", and to "forewarn them regarding the progress of future things for the fulfillment of human destiny."[58]

Throughout his life, Jesus illustrated this purpose, demonstrating all his lessons by means of his own example. Above all else, he embodied, for all to see, the supreme virtues of humility and love. From the very beginning, Jesus demonstrated this humility. As Emmanuel writes, "The manger marked the starting point for the saving lesson of the

---

In this text, Emmanuel uses the words "controlling their freedom" not in the sense of limiting or taking away their free will, but in terms of guiding or directing their use of their free will by teaching them a better way through love and compassion. In the text of this same chapter, leading up to the final section where this quoted statement is found, Emmanuel discusses the Roman Empire's expansion of its dominion by means of violence and force. He explains how the Roman family of spirits deviated from its traditional values and proved to be unappreciative of many gifts it had received.

[58] See items 3 and 4 in Chapter II of *The Gospel According to Spiritism* by Allan Kardec [original title in French: *L'Évangile Selon Le Spiritisme*, published in 1864], translation © 2008 by the International Spiritist Council, published in 2008 by the International Spiritist Council.

Christ, as if declaring that humility is the key to all the other virtues." [59] Jesus was not born into nobility but into the bare provisions of a manger. Growing up, he lived within the family setting, validating the importance of the home and obedience to one's parents. As he grew older, he did not capitalize on his true capabilities. Instead, he worked as a carpenter and made a modest living through physical labor.

When the time came for Jesus to emerge as an instructor of divine laws, he approached this task of supreme importance with the same humble heart that had directed his life to that point. In gathering his group of disciples, for example, Jesus did not rely on well-positioned friends so as to impose his doctrine through the leverage of power and influence. Instead, he chose to call upon simple men to join him in spreading his message with sincerity and faith. These followers may have questioned why Jesus refused to engage in a forceful takeover of those in political power, as he insisted on promoting change through the vehicle of compassion. Jesus, however, unwaveringly led his disciples down his path of peace, teaching devotion to his Father's will. As he went about his ministry, it was then that Jesus truly revealed not only his humility, but his love for the men and women who turned to him for instruction, healing, and inspiration. Jesus was not afraid to extend a hand to humanity. In fact, he welcomed the opportunity to reach out to the most downtrodden in society. As part of his mission to steer humankind out of the darkness and into the light, Jesus healed the sick, gave hope to sinners, comforted the weary and downtrodden, and preached to anyone willing to listen. In everything he did, Jesus exemplified God's love for all.

---

[59] See section "The Manger" in Chapter 12 of *On The Way to the Light* [original title in Portuguese: *A Caminho da Luz*], translation © 2011 by the Brazilian Spiritist Federation, published in 2011 by the International Spiritist Council.

By way of example, Jesus also taught his followers and observers about various aspects of our spiritual nature and potential. Given his degree of evolution, for example, the capability he had to foresee future events reflected his natural state, even while on Earth. Jesus also demonstrated an unseen ability to heal and cure, and he performed mysterious acts that were interpreted as miracles; in such cases, Jesus was only demonstrating the existence and action of spiritual fluids[60], as well as their submission to the character and strength of one's thought and will. Today, thanks to new information such as the details we find in Kardec's *Genesis*, we have a better explanation of such phenomena. Furthermore, we find that there are no real miracles. Everything happens in accordance with the perfect and unchanging natural laws that govern creation. We can only admire Jesus' complete knowledge of these laws. Finally, when Jesus was called to help those suffering from the influence of ill-willed spirits, his ability to command the obedience of those inferior beings demonstrated the power of his moral authority. As we learn through Spiritist teachings, this is the only authority to which such souls will adhere.

Aside from demonstrating the pathway of knowledge and love, Jesus also spent time preaching about God's laws. He offered superb wisdom and instruction to all who gathered around him, including his disciples with whom he eventually entrusted the task of carrying forth his message. Therefore, Jesus' ministry was not only one of exemplary action, but also one of teaching. One distinguishing trait that characterized his teaching was his openness to share with anyone wanting to learn from him. Ironically, in Léon Denis' book *Here and*

---

[60] See Chapter 4 "A Starting Point".

Hereafter, we can read Denis' discussion[61] of various spiritual beliefs held by civilizations that preceded Christ's incarnation among us. We see that an awareness of spirit life was present long before Jesus walked the Earth. However, as is made evident by this discussion, the great truths were often held within closed circles or reserved for privileged classes. In contrast, Christ spoke openly and shared his message with everyone, regardless of their class or background.

With great love, Jesus fulfilled his objective of making those truths accessible to all. As Denis so eloquently describes in the same book just mentioned, Jesus presented his teachings "in a fashion that the world knew not as yet, with a passionate love, a winning sweetness, a communicative faith that thawed the frosts of skepticism, and, in conquering his listeners, he made of them His devoted followers." Denis adds, "What he called 'preaching the kingdom of heaven to the lowly' simply consisted in making known to all men the facts of immortality and the existence of their common Father." [62]

One curious aspect of Jesus' teaching style is that he often spoke in figurative language, with parables and allegories. At first, this may seem counterintuitive. After all, knowing that Jesus came to clarify and enlighten, it would seem most logical to have spelled things out more directly, in the same way that advanced spirits have done through the teachings assembled under the name of Spiritism. Why, then, didn't Jesus jump straight to the point with clear and direct explanations about reincarnation, evolution, divine justice, mediumship, and so many other aspects of spirit life? Allan Kardec answers this question, explaining that the allegorical

---

[61] See sections 1 through 6 in Part 1 of *Here and Hereafter* by Léon Denis [original title in French: *Aprés La Mort*, published in 1889], translation to English by George G. Fleurot in 1909, as printed in 2005 by the Spiritist Alliance for Books.

[62] See Part 1, section 6.

form and mystical language of the Gospel were intentional. As Jesus planted seeds of knowledge concerning the loving nature of God and our need to love one another, he refrained from clearly expressing certain concepts that were beyond the capacity of his followers to understand at that time.[63] So what Christ presented, then, in principle, Spiritism has now come to complete by illustrating truths that "humans have now matured enough to comprehend."[64]

Jesus' Death on the Cross

Of course, when talking about Jesus' life on Earth, we cannot leave out his ultimate sacrifice in which his journey here among us ended in such a heartbreaking and dreadful way. Spiritists see Jesus' death on the cross as an act of love, one so great that the compassion behind it is beyond our ability to fully comprehend or appreciate. Yet, we do recognize Jesus' sacrifice in subjecting himself to this tragedy. We do not believe that this, in any way, frees us from the inevitable accountability for our actions. However, we do know that we had before us a spirit so pure that he had no evolutionary need to return to a material world. We also know that he made such sacrifices in order to ensure fulfillment of the task that God had entrusted to him. This task was to bring this planet to the splendor of spiritual purification. He did all this only to be treated, in the end, with such a thankless act of brutality and torture. Willingly born among us, Jesus lived an amazingly humble and altruistic life in this still grossly

---

[63] See, for example, *The Gospel According to Spiritism*, item 4 in Chapter I and item 3 in Chapter II.

[64] Allan Kardec in Chapter II (see item 3) of *The Gospel According to Spiritism* [original title in French: *L'Évangile Selon Le Spiritisme*, published in 1864], translation © 2008 by the International Spiritist Council, published in 2008 by the International Spiritist Council. Chapter II, item 3.

imperfect world, where he endured the disdain and persecution of those who considered themselves his enemies. Jesus voluntarily walked among men and women of the Earth to teach them about the glory of love. In his final act, meaning his faithful submission to the will of those who'd subject him to such humiliation and pain, Jesus did not atone for our sins. This was, instead, the ultimate lesson that he so selflessly left for mankind as he pleaded to his Father in heaven, "Forgive them, Father, for they know not what they do."[65]

Christian Spiritism

As Spiritists, we also refer to ourselves as Christians. We study the teachings and lessons brought to us by more advanced spirits in the spirit realm. However, we believe that Jesus called those spirits to the timely task of guiding humankind into a new and higher degree of consciousness. Through the knowledge they've shared, we better understand the meaning and importance of Jesus' lessons. We also acknowledge his supreme task of governing this beautiful world entrusted to his care. Under Jesus' careful watch, we are growing, through spiritual infancy, childhood, and adolescence, and we look forward to the phase of spiritual adulthood.

Jesus is our master, teacher, and brother. Like any young person with the deepest of love and admiration for a compassionate and successful older sibling, we look up to Jesus as our model and guide. We also know that in our hours of need, he will be there for us, ready to take our hand and help us in our difficult moments. Furthermore, upon recognizing the moral consequences of the Spiritist science

---

[65] The New Testament: Luke 23:34.

and philosophy, we seek to benefit from these lessons by actively engaging in our own spiritual development. In doing so, we find in Jesus' teachings and examples the purest and simplest expression of God's laws. Jesus himself said, "Love the Lord your God with all your heart and with all your soul and with all your mind. This is the first and greatest commandment. And the second is like it: Love your neighbor as yourself. All the Law and the Prophets hang on these two commandments."[66]

Where Spiritism helps is in the interpretation and practical application of these commandments. To illustrate that role of Spiritism and to close this chapter, I would like to share this question & answer[67] from *The Spirits' Book*. Kardec asks, "Since Jesus has already taught the true laws of God, of what value are the teachings given by the Spirits? Do they have anything to teach us?" The spirits answer:

> "Jesus' teachings were frequently allegorical and in the form of parables because he spoke according to his time and place, but today the truth must be made intelligible for all. Thus, it is necessary to explain God's laws more fully and elaborate on them because there are so few who understand them and still fewer who actually practice them. Our mission is to awaken eyes and ears in order to confound the proud and unmask the hypocrites, who display virtue and religion outwardly in order to hide their inner turpitudes. The teachings of the Spirits must be clear and without error, so that no one can feign ignorance,

---

[66] The New Testament: Matthew 22, 37–40

[67] See question and answer number 627 of *The Spirits' Book* [original title in French: *Le Livre des Espirits*, published in 1857 with 2nd edition in 1860], translation © 2006 by the International Spiritist Council, authorized edition printed in 2010 by Edicei of America.

and so that all may judge it and evaluate it with their own reason. We are in charge of preparing the Kingdom of God announced by Jesus, and that is why no one should be able to interpret the law of God according to his or her own passions or to distort the meaning of a law that is entirely love and charity."

Jesus taught and exemplified this supreme law. In fact, he is the epitome of love and charity, and as Spiritists, we turn to him as our ultimate model and guide. Spiritist teachings clarify the moral and intellectual transformation required to advance along the pathway of spiritual purification. They show us how Jesus' lessons and examples will illuminate our course and lead us to this grand destiny.

18
The Spiritist Center

Spiritists have many books to read, but how is Spiritism practiced? Do Spiritists study and/or do any other activities together? Do they have a place of worship? How do they use mediumship? If you are just coming to learn about Spiritism, these are some questions you might naturally have. At the same time, those who've had only limited contact with a Spiritist setting may not be aware of the many different ways that Spiritists come together and collaborate for their own benefit and the benefit of others.

In reality, the practice of Spiritism is, first and foremost, an individual's own reflection on Spiritism's teachings and subsequent efforts to apply them in his or her life. However, we can take that to another level. We can join like-minded individuals and reap the compound benefits of working as a group. This is what a Spiritist Center makes possible. The Spiritist Center is where Spiritists gather for study, growth, healing, and service. Just what goes on there? Let's take a look.

One of the main activities of a Spiritist center and one that is typically the first encountered by a newcomer is the public meeting. Such meetings are usually held at least once per week though there may be more. They typically involve a public presentation in which a Spiritist speaker elaborates on the subject chosen for that day. The focus may be a Spiritist idea, in particular, or a more general topic which the speaker analyzes from the Spiritist perspective. These meetings deliver a moral message, leaving listeners with points for reflection. They also clarify the meaning of Spiritist teachings and offer support for our inner transformation. The goal is to help us as we try to become better people, bring more peace into our lives, and plant seeds for greater happiness in our life to come. Following the presentation, there is usually a brief energy healing session which we refer to as *passes*. Finally, the meetings are both opened and closed with prayer. In general, this is to give thanks for the opportunity to be together, to express gratitude for the collaboration of spiritual mentors, and to ask for help for those who are in need.

Aside from these public meetings, Spiritist Centers may also offer classes or study groups for individuals interested in a deeper study of Spiritism. These sessions often present a closer look at a particular book or area of study. Such gatherings allow for a more concentrated focus in a smaller group setting. They also afford greater opportunity to ask questions, exchange ideas, and have a more personal dialogue with other participants. In addition to the meetings and study groups for adults, many centers also offer separate activities for children and youth; these often take place during the public meetings attended by the parents.

The passes that I mentioned above are a form of healing that works with the perispirit. The perispirit and its energy centers, typically known as chakras, are also the focus of diverse treatments with which you may already be familiar, including Reiki, therapeutic touch, acupuncture, and other traditional Eastern energy healing techniques. The health and harmonization of energies that flow throughout the perispirit have a direct correlation with the health of the physical body. These energies are highly susceptible to the influence of our thoughts, vibrations, and actions; positive influences have a healthy effect, and negative influences have a de-stabilizing impact. Since we are not perfect beings, we do exercise some degree of negative influence on our physical and spiritual bodies. To mitigate the adverse impacts of such influences, we should work to make our thoughts and behaviors as healthy as possible. However, these various practices of energy healing also help to re-align and re-balance our energy centers, thereby improving the flow of energies between them.

The Spiritist practice of passes looks something like the concept of the laying on of hands, though with no physical touching involved. It is understood and exercised as a donation of energies from both the material and spiritual realms. The passes are given by Spiritist workers referred to as *pass givers*. The donation of energies coming specifically from the spiritual realm is made possible through the collaboration of spiritual benefactors. In this case, the pass givers serve as channels for the transmission of those energies to the recipient. Pass givers may also donate energies of their own as part of the transmission.

Another way for us to receive healing and restorative energies is through what Spiritists call *fluidified water*. This is simply water that spiritual benefactors infuse with properties supportive to our well-being. It is usually offered following the donation of passes.

There are many concepts behind this extremely brief mention of energy healing – from the perispirit and spiritual fluids to the action of discarnate spirits and the very principles of fluidic therapy. I did, however, want to provide an introduction to the topic; this way, should you ever visit a Spiritist Center and have the opportunity to receive passes, you will have some idea of what is involved. Through other resources, you can learn about these concepts in more detail[68].

Aside from these studying and healing activities, Spiritist Centers offer additional ways to receive help and to

---

[68] See, for example, the ExploreSpiritism.com website; go to the *Science* section and find the menu topic entitled *Fluidic Therapy*.

be of help to others. In some Centers, you will find a service called *fraternal counseling*. To individuals facing a difficult time in their lives, this service offers a confidential, one-on-one conversation with someone who is both willing to listen without judgment and capable of suggesting a viewpoint based on Spiritist knowledge. In these dialogues, one can find support, hope, and a new perspective. In addition, this support is typically accompanied by energy healing sessions.

Another example of Spiritist service and assistance is the community outreach work that Spiritist Centers often engage in. These activities are open to any members who wish to join. Volunteering through such programs is another great way for participants to give of their time, energy, and love to make a difference in the lives of others.

Finally, the practice of mediumship is another very important function of the Spiritist Center. Like any activity in the Center, mediumship is practiced for the dignified purposes of service. It is also another tool to aid in our progress. We do not, therefore, have entertaining séances, readings, or the like. We do not use mediumship to satisfy curiosity, predict the future, or provide a form of amusement. When spiritual benefactors reach out to us through mediums, they do so for the sake of offering words of comfort, inspiration, or education. They also wish to aid and support us in our noble efforts, and they aim to steer us away from danger or mistakes. Countless beneficial messages and communications, as well as entire books, have been received with these objectives. There are also spiritual mentors who offer guidance specific to the operation of the Center.

There is one particular practice that is rather unique to Spiritism. It reflects the Spiritist beliefs regarding the application of mediumship for charitable purposes. This practice involves meetings held for the purpose of counseling unhappy or suffering, discarnate spirits, as well as for treating cases of obsession[69]. As you'll recall, I mentioned a little about this in a previous chapter[70]. This work is always carried out in collaboration with spiritual mentors and benefactors. As for the discarnate souls in need of assistance, they may be alone in their suffering, or they may be acting, out of pain, with the intention to bring danger or harm to others. In the Spiritist Center, they are always treated with compassion. In other words, we do not perform "exorcisms" or treat them in any way as demons. Instead, we see them as brothers and sisters in need of help. Just as if we were counseling another person, face to face, we treat these spirits with love. We encourage them to see things from another perspective, in which they may realize that there is a better way to resolve their problems. We help them gain control of their emotions, and we show them a path to peace. Finally, we enable their understanding of God's compassion. When applicable, we help them discover the liberating effect of forgiveness.

---

[69] As noted in a previous chapter, *obsession* refers to the persistent and negative influence of one spirit over another – in this context, a discarnate spirit over an incarnate one. The counseling of an unhappy or suffering spirit involves a therapeutic dialogue between that discarnate spirit (who communicates through a medium) and an incarnate advisor, or counselor. This counselor listens with compassion, and in collaboration with workers from the spiritual realm, he or she offers supportive fraternal assistance to the troubled spirit. Through this process, the unhappy spirit begins to see his or her situation differently and finds a renewed sense of understanding, relief, and hope; this does not necessarily happen in just one session and may in fact take place over the course of several mediumship sessions. For more information, see the ExploreSpiritism.com website; go to the Science section and find the menu topic entitled *Obsession* (including *Cure & Treatment for Obsession*).

[70] See Chapter 15 "Beware of Bad Company".

Now that you are familiar with some of the main activities of a Spiritist Center, let's look at some important points regarding the way Spiritist Centers are operated. One key aspect involves the extensiveness of the volunteer work that takes place in order make the functions of a Spiritist Center possible. From cleaning the facility or taking care of the bookstore to serving as the highest level administrator, such efforts are most typically[71] made without financial reward. In addition, such work is quite often performed by people who have regular paid jobs outside the Center. While such forms of participation and service do require a sense of duty and responsibility, these volunteer contributions are truly a labor of love. Aside from this, Spiritist Centers have no ordained ministers or preachers of any kind or of any other name. Those who perform services within a Spiritist Center are people who are qualified by the appropriate level of study and skills, as well as the willingness to serve and the dedication needed to be a reliable resource.

The love that goes into the running of a Spiritist Center does not come from the incarnate contributors alone. It is our generous and supportive benefactors from the spirit realm who truly make it possible with their guidance and collaboration. Often times, they are helping in ways we are not even aware of. In any case, they are a part of every form of work that goes on inside the Center. They even carry out forms of service that take place strictly in the spiritual plane. Such activities are invisible to most people since the vast majority only see what goes on in the physical plane. For

---

[71] As previously noted, in some cases, there may be individuals who are paid for labor involved with work including book publishing, janitorial maintenance, cooking, babysitting, transportation, etc. However, this is not in most Centers and if found, it is more likely to be in those locations that have become large facilities. It will not include work done by speakers and other instructors, the Center's administrators, mediums, pass-givers, etc.

example, they help to improve the quality of energies inside that environment. In addition, they bring discarnate spirits who would benefit from our classes and lectures to listen to those meetings. They also bring unhappy and suffering spirits to receive help through the mediumship services. Sometimes there are even hospitals and other facilities that exist within the spiritual dimension of a Spiritist Center. It is all truly amazing and certainly fascinating to learn more about.

This spiritual dimension of the Spiritist Center is significant. To those already going to a Spiritist Center, I strongly encourage you to understand it. The details involved reveal the importance of being vigilant of our behavior when we are there. Our thoughts and actions impact the subtle energies so carefully prepared by dedicated and benevolent spirits. The energy and environment inside the Center is extremely important, not only to the Center's functioning in our material realm, but also to the work being done in the invisible plane. For this reason, we must treat the Center and its environment with our utmost respect.

The Spiritist Center is a place where we can study and grow, acquire knowledge, gain valuable insights, and exchange ideas. In addition, we can find fraternal assistance and receive help with healing and restoration. We can also enjoy pleasant conversation, make friends, and build positive relationships. At Spiritist Centers, we find numerous opportunities to work and serve. Finally, the Spiritist Center affords a setting in which individuals from both the spiritual and material worlds consciously come together to collaborate in the study and application of Spiritist teachings. It is truly a special place.

19
The Perspective From "Up Here"

Picture yourself somewhere in this world enjoying a beautiful landscape. You grab your camera and try to take some snapshots because you want to share this wonder with your friends and family. When you go to show the pictures, no matter how great they are, you still find yourself disappointed. The photos just don't do that beautiful landscape justice. Never fails, right? Our peripheral vision and turning heads allow us to take in the entire scene all at once. The average camera, however, just cannot capture the same view. So what we end up with in the photo is literally just a snapshot of the bigger picture that actually exists.

In *The Spirits' Book*, Allan Kardec comments on the spirits' answers to questions about the purpose of destructive natural calamities. He writes, "If we could elevate ourselves, through thought, so as to encompass all humankind from a single glance, these calamities would seem no more than passing storms in the destiny of the world."[72] Truth is, whether we're talking about great acts of nature that suddenly turn lives upside down, or a passing circumstance that leaves pain and struggle in its path, this elevated perspective cited in the spirits' answer is applicable to all of them. When we're *in the moment*, whether that lasts a day or a lifetime, our vision of a situation is naturally restricted. This is especially true when we are incarnated and living in a material world such as our own. However, if we were to

---

[72] See question and answer #4 in *The Spirits' Book* by Allan Kardec [original title in French: *Le Livre des Espirits*, published in 1857 with 2nd edition in 1860], translation © 2006 by the International Spiritist Council, authorized edition printed in 2010 by Edicei of America.

somehow rise above the more immediate circumstances and look down on them so as to see what lies behind, ahead, and all around, the view would be very different.

Aside from the picture-taking example, there are numerous other analogies we could use to demonstrate this concept. For instance, suppose you were looking down on a hiker climbing through a forest-covered mountain. At any given time, the hiker would see only his immediate surroundings. You, on the other hand, would see how far he'd climbed, any obstacles in his path, and how far he was from reaching the top. In the same sense, picture the GPS and mapping applications that we use for navigating on roadways. As we're driving, we can zoom right in on our present location and confirm what we see around us. On the other hand, we can also zoom out to get a broader view of that which is not visible from our physical location. In addition, we can identify alternate routes and destinations. Finally, picture a cross-stitching design in the making. If we could only look at the cloth from the underside, all we would see is the chaotic and seemingly random crisscrossing of many differently colored threads. However, as we watch the view from above, we see how the various pieces of thread combine perfectly to reveal a single, coherent picture.

The contrasting viewpoints demonstrated by the above examples are analogous to the contrast between a limited, single life view and a much broader, more revealing perspective in which we see ourselves as immortal, evolving, and reincarnating human spirits. Our more advanced spiritual benefactors observe us from the latter point of view. This is how they are able to give us trustworthy guidance as they celebrate our successes and lament our failures without despair. When they witness our setbacks, they know we will one day redeem ourselves from our mistakes. When we are in the spirit realm in between incarnations, we often have a better glimpse into this bigger picture. To some degree, we see the continuity of events and experiences that have played out over our multiple material lifetimes. However, at the present moment, given our stage of evolution and our current condition as incarnate spirits, we typically do not see ourselves from such a vantage point. We do not have a detailed view of our spiritual history. In most cases, we also have no real awareness about our ultimate destiny. Still, this does not mean that a greater notion of our spiritual nature is unavailable. To the contrary, Spiritism offers a great deal of wisdom concerning the connections between our spiritual past, present and future. This form of enlightenment helps us to broaden our horizons and envision life from a more elevated perspective. Once that happens, we begin to see our existence in a new light.

One of the first changes to happen as we zoom out on our view of life may be that we realize it is so much bigger than we had ever conceptualized. Do you know that feeling you get when you stand on the beach and look out into the ocean, or when you gaze up at the sky on a clear and starry night, and you feel almost overwhelmed by the immensity of this world around us? Well this sensation is even greater. With a newfound understanding that we have lived many lives before this one and have many more yet to come, this lifetime we're in now suddenly becomes as if it were "just a day", a spec in time, when compared to all of eternity. We begin to appreciate the transitory nature of our present circumstances. In this, we find a greater will to tolerate them patiently.

This patience might be far less than unshakeable if it were not for the complementary understanding of how our present lives relate to our former ones. Through Spiritist teachings, we discover how our entrance into this world marked the inheritance of who we were, what we did, and the choices we made in our former incarnations. As I've discussed in previous chapters, these revelations from the Spiritist science and philosophy demonstrate that nothing happens without reason or just cause. This is particularly comforting when considering our times of great difficulty, challenge, hardship, and pain. Rather than questioning the fairness of our position or the innumerable disparities in our world, we understand that divine justice employs nothing but compassionate measures to aid in our spiritual transformation. By no means are we spared from the need to benefit from our trials. We must learn to endure them with courage and faith, and by the same token, it is our collective duty to compassionately help one another through these trials. It is precisely through such efforts that suffering educates and enables progress. Fortunately, in Spiritism we find great insight in the testimonies of other souls who were once where we are now and who lovingly embrace us with their words of encouragement. Through their support, we find inspiration and vision. They illustrate to us that suffering is only temporary and that a greater happiness lies just beyond the horizon.

    This broadened vision of our future also comforts us by assuring that we have the extent of eternity to live all our dreams. If, for example, we've encountered the disappointment of not having the opportunity to pursue the career we desire, have the family we want desperately to be a part of, develop a talent that we greatly admire, visit places that we crave to know first-hand, or experience a freedom that we may long for, we can find solace in the fact that this will be possible in the future. We must have patience and faith, but this perspective quiets our feelings of urgency, allowing us to focus on whatever we are called to accomplish in this life so that we may be free to pursue those dreams later on.

In some cases, this elevated perspective triggers a wake-up call inside us. We realize that any enjoyable and celebrated conditions that we may experience today are not guaranteed to be part of our life in the future. This is not referring just to the afterlife, but to future incarnations as well. If we fail to appreciate such blessings, or we act, in spite of these divine gifts, with selfishness and greed, we thereby sign ourselves up for future lessons in gratitude, humility, and charity. With this understanding, we also become cognizant of how natural laws establish an unfailing accountability for the way we use our free will. While the law of action and reaction applies equally to both the good and bad choices we make, the fact that it will manifest well beyond this physical lifetime can be an eye-opening gift. Those who take advantage of such knowledge become more vigilant of their thoughts and actions, and they make conscious efforts to change their ways for the better.

Perhaps it goes without saying, but the opposite circumstances are also true. A greater awareness of our spiritual life reinforces any positive efforts we are already making. It gives us the strength to follow both the guidance of our conscience and the instruction of moral teachings. It illustrates just how sublime life will become if we remain persistent in those noble and dignified efforts.

Truthfully, this elevated perspective sheds light on so many aspects of life. Birth and death are two more examples. Let's look first at birth. Once we see life from a higher viewpoint, the concept of birth is no longer the beginning of life, even if we include fertilization and conception in our understanding of it. Birth is merely a continuation of life, representing the transition of a spirit into the temporary, incarnate state. Through Spiritist texts, we learn about all the planning that actually goes on in the spirit realm long before the formation of that physical body begins! It is quite fascinating when you begin to read about how our spiritual benefactors assist in this planning. No less intriguing is their involvement in the subsequent physical processes that take place in the material world. At times, they are called upon to help ensure the successful gestation and birth of the newborn baby, which is, in reality, the return of an immortal spirit to this temporary life in the physical realm.[73]

Just as birth is not the start of life, physical death (the opposite process) is not the end. It is merely liberation from the physical body, representing the return of the immortal spirit to life in the spiritual realm. In Spiritist texts, we encounter depictions of how spiritual benefactors help disincarnating spirits with this process – from the loosening of ties between the spiritual and physical bodies to the process of awakening and re-adaptation in the spiritual world.[74] To have such awareness changes the way we think and talk about death, for we see it more naturally. As a consequence, the way we behave upon the return of our loved ones to the spiritual realm also changes.[75] Once we truly understand how our spiritual life continues after physical death, the significance of

---

[73] A recommendable resource for learning more about this is the book *Missionaries of the Light* by spirit author André Luiz and medium Francisco Cândido Xavier. This is part of the "Life in the Spirit World" book series.

[74] A recommended resource for learning more about this is the book *Workers of the Life Eternal* by spirit author André Luiz and medium Francisco Cândido Xavier. This is part of the "Life in the Spirit World" book series.

[75] For those interested, I recommend the book *Who Is Afraid of Death* by Spiritist author Richard Simonetti. This book explains the concept of death and several related topics from the perspective of Spiritism. It presents these subjects in an informative yet very accessible language. The book is an easy read that helps us understand how this process is a very natural part of our spiritual existence, and it provides valuable explanations and answers related to questions that concern many people.

that awareness is extraordinarily meaningful. Allan Kardec captured this idea well, in the book *Heaven and Hell*, when he wrote:

> "To the degree that humans better comprehend the future life, the fear of death decreases. Once their earthly mission becomes clear, they calmly, resignedly and fearlessly await the end. Certainty about the future life gives them another course for their thoughts, another aim for their labors. Prior to this certainty, they only labored with an eye on the present. With this certainty, however, they labor with an eye on the future, although without neglecting the present since they know that the future depends on the good or evil direction they take in the present. The certainty of meeting their friends again after death, of reactivating the relationships they had on Earth, of *not losing one single fruit of their labor*, of unceasingly growing in intelligence and toward perfection, gives them the patience to endure and the courage to bear the transitory weariness of earthly life. The solidarity they find between the living and the dead enables them to understand the solidarity they must establish on Earth, where fraternity and charity have a purpose and a reason for being, both in the present and in the future."[76]

I'd like to mention one more example of how teachings like those of Spiritism alter the way we interpret life. It is hinted at in Kardec's statement where he spoke of the

---

[76] See Chapter II, Item 3, in Part 1 of *Heaven and Hell* by Allan Kardec [original title in French: *Le Ciel Et L'Enfer*, published in 1865], translation © 2006 by the International Spiritist Council, published in 2008 by the International Spiritist Council.

"solidarity [we] must establish on earth". More specifically, I refer to the many relationships that become a part of our lives. It may seem as though the events that put us in contact with one another are merely random occurrences, whether desirable or not. However, that is not actually the case, especially with our more significant relationships, those of the family being a primary example. All of these relationships and interactions, as well as other experiences in life, present us with the precise circumstances needed for both our individual and collective spiritual progress.

In theory, this is easy enough to understand, at least on the surface. In fact, various religions or philosophies may teach something similar. However, if we try to dig deeper, we may start asking questions about where these needs come from and why the spiritual goals for one person's life may be so drastically different from those of another. Now we're back at that starting point where we can only answer those questions by bringing in the existence of reincarnation and spiritual evolution. In other words, we're "zooming out" to encompass both past and present. In these realities of spiritual life, we find the source of our diversified needs and the framework for the planning of circumstances designed to help meet them.

Many of our learning experiences put us in contact with complete strangers, fellow souls who we encounter for the first time. Even so, there are typically individuals in our lives who share in our spiritual history. They were with us in one or more previous incarnations, and it is not without reason that we find ourselves together again. Often times, these reencounters are designed to help us work out differences from the past so that we may mend broken relationships, establish forgiveness for transgressions, achieve success where we once failed, or restore bonds of love and affection. Meanwhile, we don't always reunite to make amends. We may come together to accomplish a special task, to strengthen fraternal ties, or to join forces to help someone else who is also a part of our spiritual history.

When it comes to reuniting spirits with a common past, the relationships established in the home are often the means of facilitating these opportunities, thus adding another layer of special importance to our *family constellation*, as aptly described by the spirit author Joanna de Ângelis.[77] Outside our families, there are innumerable other circumstances through which we can and do become intentionally reunited with individuals from our former lives.

Regardless of whether the other souls in our lives come from within our families or outside of them, and irrespective of whether we know them from the past or have met them only in this lifetime, our relationships most certainly serve as opportunities for moral progress. Through Spiritism, we learn how to identify those opportunities. We are encouraged to take advantage of them by paying close attention to our mental, emotional, and behavioral conduct and by making the conscious effort to approach all our relationships with the spirit of charity and love.

Though the totality of illustrations we could discuss is much more inclusive, I have included some important examples to demonstrate the advantage of looking down on life from an elevated perspective, one that connects our past, present, and future. Spiritism is, without a doubt, an excellent

---

[77] *Family Constellation* is the title of a book written by the spirit author Joanna de Ângelis and psychographed by the medium Divaldo Franco. In this book, Joanna discusses the different roles and relationships that make up a family unit. She offers insight on various aspects of family dynamics, both in light of the Spiritist teachings and in consideration of many issues faced by families in today's world. English translation © 2010 by Centro Espírita Camino da Redenção, published by Livraría Espírita Alvorada Editora [original title in Portuguese, *Constelação Familiar*, © 2008].

tool for looking at life from such a vantage point. To close this chapter, I will leave you with an affirmation from Allan Kardec found in *The Gospel According to Spiritism*. He writes:

> "Spiritism broadens one's thoughts and opens up new horizons. Instead of this narrow and small-minded view that concentrates on the present life, which makes the instant that one passes on Earth the unique and fragile pivot of the eternal future, Spiritism shows that this life is only one link in the harmonious and magnificent whole of the Creator's work. Spiritism also demonstrates the solidarity that interconnects all the existences of one being, all beings of the same world, and all beings of all worlds."[78]

---

[78] See item 7 in Chapter II of *The Gospel According to Spiritism* by Allan Kardec [original title in French: *L'Évangile Selon Le Spiritisme*, published in 1864], translation © 2008 by the International Spiritist Council, published in 2008 by the International Spiritist Council.

20
The Only Way

In spite of this final chapter's title, I will not conclude my book-long invitation to study Spiritism by urging you to become a Spiritist *or else*. I will not tell you that *Spiritism* is the only way to peace and happiness. Often times, we hear people refer to the word *salvation*. Regardless of the language used to express the thought, we all, in one way or another, are speaking of this same desired destiny. If we are seeking salvation, then we are looking for some kind of rescue or deliverance. And from what are we seeking this deliverance, if not from our present or future pains and suffering? Where we differ is in the definition of how to achieve this goal and, consequently, who will be so rewarded. Some religions proclaim to be in sole possession of the truth about how to achieve true and everlasting peace; yet, if a doctrine admits only a single lifetime in which one may have the chance to earn this "golden ticket", then woe to those who do not do so before their time is up.

Spiritism makes no such claims. Look, for example, at question # 982 in *The Spirits' Book.* It inquires, "Is it necessary to make a profession of faith in Spiritism and to believe in spirit manifestations, in order to ensure our well-being in the next life?", to which the reply is given, "If that were so, then all those who do not believe in them, or who have not had the opportunity to learn anything about them, would be disinherited, which is absurd. Only the good ensures one's future well-being. The good is always good, whatever path leads to it."⁷⁹ Furthermore, in the book *What is Spiritism*, Allan Kardec defines the best of all religions as:

> "that which teaches only what conforms to God's goodness and justice; which entails the broadest, most sublime idea about God and does not lessen him by attributing human narrow-mindedness and passions to him; which renders people good and virtuous and teaches them all to love each other as brothers and sisters; which condemns every wrong done to one's neighbor; which does not authorize injustice under any form or pretext; which does not prescribe anything contrary to the immutable laws of nature, for God cannot contradict himself; whose clergy embody the best example of goodness, charity, and morality; the one that best pursues the struggle against selfishness and least flatters people's pride and vanity; and lastly, in whose name the least amount of evil is committed, for a good religion cannot be the pretext for any evil whatsoever. It must not leave any door open to it, either directly or by interpretation." ⁸⁰

Spiritism is grounded in the spirits' teachings about evolution, free will, and accountability, as well as in their guidance about how to live so as to earn merit for a better future. As such, it stands outside of dogma and segregation, ensuring us that time is never up. Eventually, we will all attain purification, which will bring us pure joy. Spiritism

---

[79] See question # 982 of *The Spirits' Book* by Allan Kardec [original title in French: *Le Livre des Espirits*, published in 1857 with 2nd edition in 1860], translation © 2006 by the International Spiritist Council, authorized edition printed in 2010 by Edicei of America.

[80] *What is Spiritism* by Allan Kardec, published in 1859; English translation © 2010 by the International Spiritist Council, as published in 2011 by the International Spiritist Council.

simply defines the "only way" as *love*. This is a pure love that must be learned and lived, a point made very clear throughout Kardec's works. In fact, one of the greatest and simplest maxims of Spiritism is that "without charity, there is no salvation"[81]. Charity is defined as "benevolence toward everyone, indulgence toward the imperfection of others, and forgiveness for offenses."[82] Lest we not be mistaken; there are no external sources of salvation. There is only limitless time and opportunity, as granted by our merciful Creator, to achieve it. That all-important love, essential to our complete happiness, is instilled within us like a seed of consciousness. It can only grow and manifest in all its beauty by way of our own labor. Progress and transformation require effort, but the reward for this effort goes far beyond the merely compensatory.

One of the key attributes that lends Spiritism such authority to make these claims about the significance of love and compassion is the fact that it does not look at science and religion in isolation from one another. In one holistic picture, Spiritism explains the nature of both spirits and worlds, demonstrating how their evolution takes place through the vehicle of intellectual and moral progress, always in accordance with divine, natural law. In Spiritism, science and religion walk not in fear of or in opposition to one another, but rather hand-in-hand in a mutually supportive relationship.

---

[81] See item 5 in Chapter XV of *The Gospel According to Spiritism* by Allan Kardec [original title in French: *L'Évangile Selon Le Spiritisme*, published in 1864], translation © 2008 by the International Spiritist Council, published in 2008 by the International Spiritist Council.

[82] This is the spirits' answer to the question "What is the true meaning of the word charity as Jesus understood it?". See question # 886 in *The Spirits' Book* by Allan Kardec [original title in French: *Le Livre des Espirits*, published in 1857 with 2nd edition in 1860], translation © 2006 by the International Spiritist Council, authorized edition printed in 2010 by Edicei of America.

Through this relationship, unfailing love emerges as the key to our salvation.

It is quite encouraging to see the collection of empirical *spiritual* evidence now mounting as the scientific world slowly opens to the study of concepts already taught, for centuries, by various religions and philosophies of the world. These concepts are mainly in areas related to the existence and immortality of the soul, as well as the faculty of mediumship, the existence of reincarnation, and the ability to remember past lives. However, among the more contemporary studies, we've also seen an increasing degree of dialogue about the need for compassion, as well as a growing number of efforts in the scientific investigation and analysis of morality and its impact on our well-being.

These findings have supported age-old philosophical and religious arguments, ones claiming that gratitude, compassion, kindness, and selflessness are all good for our mental, physical, and social well-being. What's still lacking is the integrated analysis that demonstrates why all of that matters, not just for today or tomorrow, but beyond this life and into eternity. Such an explanation only comes when we acknowledge our spiritual nature and begin to recognize the bigger-picture design of our wise and just Creator. At that point, we will find that all those admirable virtues are, first and foremost, the very elements necessary for our spiritual well-being. In turn, the effects of our spiritual well-being naturally spill over into our mental, physical, and social condition.

Not only does the Spiritist knowledge explain how to improve our future condition; it also answers questions about how we got to where we are today. For example, we might ask the following: If we are somehow intended to be compassionate, by design, then why are there certain individuals who are so much more, or less, naturally inclined toward compassion than others? Why are there people who suffer so much more, or less, than others from forces beyond their control? And how can it be that we find some courageous individuals who demonstrate tremendous compassion, even in the face of remarkable suffering, thus inspiring awe and admiration in those around them? Only in an evolutionary view, combining both science and spirituality to tie the various pieces together through reincarnation, can we find answers to those questions.

We can certainly find some relatively progressive ideas in current pockets of religious thought. Meanwhile, science is moving toward its own spiritual breakthrough. Spiritism, on the other hand, has been teaching us about the perspective found where science and religion meet ever since the Spiritist codification's inception in the mid to late 1800s. Therefore, whenever the occasional question arises as to whether Kardec and his work are outdated, I will adamantly argue that such is not the case. How could it be if Spiritism contains both the theory and evidence to answer the very questions people are still asking regarding some of the most fundamental aspects of life? Kardec is not outdated. He was ahead of his time and is still relevant now, in fact very much so.

Ironically, we recently saw the passing of our most famous astronaut, Neil Armstrong, the first man to walk on the moon. This is a man whose career led him to take part in such an important, historical event, but whose soul has now left the Earth for more than just a round-trip mission to space and back. As I reflect on the depth of knowledge in Spiritism and its relevance to the progress of humanity, I can't help but hear an echo of Armstrong's famous, resonating words pronounced as he first ventured out onto the moon's surface:

"One small step for man. One giant leap for mankind". Though I'd dare say that the discovery of both the human spirit and the reality of spirit life is not a small, but rather a huge step for man, the day these truths become mainstream knowledge will most certainly be a day that will take humankind by leaps and bounds into a new era of enlightenment.

This widespread enlightenment will give birth to a newfound appreciation for the moral responsibilities inherent to our spiritual existence. Spiritism teaches about these responsibilities while demonstrating how they are the solution to our eradication of suffering and sorrow – both individual and collective. Spiritist texts, like *The Gospel According to Spiritism* and many other helpful resources, provide depth to this concept through practical explanations and clarifications. They motivate and enable us to apply the concept of charity to all aspects of our lives. Through them, we comprehend what it truly means to give love and receive love. Furthermore, we understand why love – for God, ourselves, and one another – is the only way to achieve our salvation.

◊ ◊ ◊

Through the great, evolutionary school of life, we inevitably acquire a progressively deeper understanding about the meaning of love. At this point, our two greatest obstacles to moral progress, according to Spiritism, are pride and selfishness. It should come as no surprise that to clear these obstacles from our path, we can only do so through humility and compassion[83].

---

[83] For example, see item 5 in Chapter XV of *The Gospel According to Spiritism*.

Humility is what allows us to see ourselves for who we really are, with all our strengths and weaknesses. It also allows us to focus on achieving the true joy of victory over our own imperfections, rather than relishing a fleeting and deceptive pleasure in the false sense of superiority or the judgment and criticism of others. Likewise, it is only through humility that we see ourselves as equals before God. In other words, we see ourselves and one another through God's eyes. From this view, we understand that we all have the same origin and destiny, the same need to overcome vulnerability of will and fragility of faith, the same obligation to pick ourselves up when we fall, and the same duty to learn from our mistakes. We also recognize that we each have the same longing, capacity, and potential for love, and that it is God's will for each of us to one day experience and embody love in its greatest form.

Through humility, we recognize that hurtful actions stem from pain and ignorance, and this understanding strengthens our ability to practice patience, tolerance, and forgiveness. Humility is also the virtue by which we accept God's will and recognize his wisdom and mercy. We therefore acknowledge that in our limited perspective we don't always know what is right for us, and we recognize that God's laws are designed to look out for our best interests. In this way, we become increasingly better at avoiding actions that cause delays in our progress, and we begin to take advantage of opportunities to learn, heal, and grow.

If humility is the remedy for pride, then our ailments stemming from selfishness and greed require the healing change toward ways of solidarity and compassion. Divine law makes it our duty as brothers, sisters, and children of one God to respect and help one another. Those higher on the ladder of progress must lend a helping hand to those who follow behind them. Those who find themselves in a comfortable position – socially, financially, or otherwise – should be grateful and give thanks for such blessings. Rather than believing or wanting to show themselves to be in any way superior and more deserving, they should reach out in fraternal efforts and in absence of judgment to improve the plight of those less fortunate. Those who find themselves exceptionally endowed with wealth, power, talent, or fame can be sure that they have great responsibilities, for even such gifts can represent trials or commitments that come with a great deal of accountability. Meanwhile, those with much less money, skill, or authority should not feel that they are without duty to give something of themselves; remember the story of the widow's mite[84]. Likewise, as we find emphatically clarified in Spiritist teachings, expressions of compassion and acts of charity do not exclusively take the form of material donations. There are a great number of ways for any of us to be more caring toward one another, including loving words of encouragement, support, or advice; a donation of time in fraternal service; an effort to tolerate, understand, or forgive; and the willingness to exercise patience, kindness, mercy, and so on.

Through various teachings about virtue and ethical progress, it becomes evident that while there is merit in doing no wrong, it is not enough to simply cause no harm, at least for those looking to enjoy the rewards of greater progress. Likewise, we cannot selfishly close our eyes and remain indifferent to the misfortunes and suffering of our neighbors. The divine laws call on us to look beyond our own wants and

---

[84] The New Testament: Mark 12:41–44 and Luke 21:1–4. In this biblical account, a poor widow gives to the church only 2 coins of the least value possible (called mites), yet this is all she has to her name; Jesus explains that this donation is more valuable (in terms of merit) than the less charitable donations of leftovers made by the most wealthy.

interests, and it is only through compassion that we are willing to consider and take action in light of the thoughts, feelings, and needs of those around us. The more we are able to think and act in the absence of self-interest, the more natural it becomes for us to make sacrifices for the sake of keeping peace, spreading joy, or easing pain. Ironically, this kind of *love in action* has such a positive effect on our well-being that once we consciously engage in acts of benevolence and charity, we soon discover the wonderful feeling of making a difference for others, whether by drying tears, easing burdens, inciting hope, or bringing forth happiness. The need for this kind of solidarity is essential within our homes, our communities, and our cultures and nations, as well as on a global scale. At the same time, the relevance extends beyond the population presently living on our planet to include that of future generations. It is only through the diminishing of pride and selfishness that our planet will follow its evolutionary course to become a world of less suffering and greater harmony.

While humility and compassion are both intimately entwined with the virtue of forgiveness, it is worth making special mention of this particular expression of love. It is one thing to demonstrate compassion toward those we easily deem worthy of our affection, or even toward strangers with whom we sympathize. It is yet another to open our hearts toward those who have caused us pain. In such circumstances, it is helpful to remember, if we believe in Spiritist teachings, that we are never truly victims in life, at least not innocent ones. Spiritism enlightens us about the potential causes (whether in the present or in a past life) that may have resulted in such circumstances. From Spiritism, we also learn about severe cases in which rivaling spirits spend multiple lifetimes going back and forth between the roles of victim and transgressor.

In order to break such cycles, we must resist temptations toward resentment and revenge. Forgiveness is not a weak act of obedience. On the contrary, it is a tremendous display of courage and strength. Furthermore, while we may think we are forgiving for the sake of our transgressor, we are actually the first to benefit. This is because we are the first to suffer the effects of our own anger and bitterness. Forgiveness, therefore, is not only an act of compassion. It is actually a gift through which we allow ourselves to be free from the harmful effects of such destructive emotions.

Aside from this well-known yet under-appreciated benefit of forgiveness, Spiritism also gives us many illustrations of how God and our spiritual benefactors have everything under their careful watch and control. It is simply wiser to leave things in their hands. Additionally, by the insights gained through such illustrations, we begin to develop a sense of compassion toward those who make lamentable choices in the use of their free will. We actually pity them, knowing the kind of pain they are liable to face when they become conscious of the significance of their actions. Ultimately, forgiveness is the only way that we can achieve both individual and collective liberation from the imprisoning cycles of animosity and hatred. This freedom, in turn, is the only way we can begin to construct new and lasting ties of solidarity and love.

◊ ◊ ◊

These actions and the approaches to life that I have mentioned focus primarily on how we relate to those around us. However, harmony in life comes with balance. Looking within and caring for our own being is just as important as looking outward in consideration of those around us. For certain, we also have the right and the duty to love ourselves. This does not mean we should do so in an exaggerated or prideful way, but rather with humility and appreciation for the gift of life.

To begin with, we have the right to seek happiness! If true happiness is not *of* this world, it is because the world we live in reflects our current stage of evolution and thereby offers the conditions presently needed for our spiritual progress. However, that does not mean that there is no happiness *in* this world, for indeed we do find it. I'm not referring to fleeting pleasures that satisfy the ego. I'm talking about lasting sources of joy that touch the soul, such as fulfilling relationships, love and laughter, the beauty of nature, the appreciation of simplicity, the peace of innocence, the satisfaction of accomplishment, and the gratification of giving. The key point is that happiness only exists in this world because of those who create it. Happiness is not something that can be bought in the market or produced in a lab. It must be nourished from within the individual, whereby it then grows and multiplies when shared. In order for happiness to come from within, compassion is an absolute must. We've already reviewed how compassion toward others benefits our well-being. Compassion toward ourselves is no less important. This is the only way we will achieve the kind of happiness that is both lasting and radiant.

There are a number of ways in which we can treat ourselves with compassion. One way is through forgiveness. While we cannot avoid the remorse we feel when our conscience alerts us to our mistakes, we will accomplish nothing by imprisoning ourselves in relentlessly punishing thoughts. We must be willing to continue. We must learn from our errors and march forward, trusting in God's love through which we will have the eventual opportunity to make things right. Likewise, we should do what we can to minimize the effects of our misguided actions. Let us be clear; the school of life does not always teach us through expiation and redemption. It is full of diverse opportunities for us to simply develop and expand upon the beauty and potential of our transforming souls! Innumerable experiences offer us chances to mature and grow. They empower us to develop strength, self-respect and self-worth, to demonstrate bravery and courage, and to push our limits. They invite us to chase our dreams, express our creativity, and explore our imagination. These experiences are all part of our evolutionary voyage through which we gradually overcome weaknesses, enhance our capabilities, and develop virtues. Furthermore, though we must work hard, we are, in fact, allowed to have fun and take time to rest. Ultimately, it is only through kindness toward ourselves, balanced with our responsibilities toward others, that we will take advantage of these opportunities when life presents them.

Taking care of ourselves also means that we must be good stewards of our minds, bodies, and souls. In addition to the more obvious forms of diet and exercise, stress management, and spiritual nourishment, there are direct implications for all our thoughts, actions, choices, and behaviors. These are all concepts which Spiritism helps us to understand and apply. Aside from that, there are numerous non-Spiritist resources that offer tools for managing the challenges of life. By all means, we should take advantage of them. However, once we grasp how everything we think and do has corresponding repercussions, whether now or in the future, this changes how we see and approach life. It shapes what we value today, thereby attracting what we will experience tomorrow. It even makes us more willing to intervene, with more conscious thought, in our own actions, reactions, and decisions. The latter efforts become an expression of self-directed kindness, a requisite to earn merit for health and well-being, even if this consequence does not fully manifest until a subsequent incarnation.

Aside from stewardship, compassion toward ourselves also calls for a good dose of tough love. By this, I refer to the ways in which we handle problems, withstand sorrows, and endure hardships because life does have its share of obstacles and trials. Spiritism teaches us about the ways in which these circumstances can come about, assuring us that no matter their cause or purpose, there is always an explanation behind them. Furthermore, what is most important is our effort to endure suffering and pain without rebellion or despair. This kind of resignation does not mean that we should sit back in indifference. Nor should we accept our situation in a spirit of defeat or from a feeling of abandonment. Instead, we must seek the courage to accept circumstances that, for whatever reason, are beyond our control or ability to change. I call this tough love because it requires hard work, perseverance, and sacrifice for the sake of our own benefit. Although it offers many ways to help us with these efforts, Spiritism is not the only viable resource for such support. Any tool or belief that gives one the ability to face adversity or suffering with comprehension and resolute faith is valid in that regard. In the end, to lift the burdens that hinder our progress and to clear our path to freedom and happiness, we must do so by bearing our trials with resignation, determination, and trust in divine providence.

◊ ◊ ◊

In *The Gospel According to Spiritism*, Kardec concludes that humility and charity are the sole path to salvation[85]. Spiritism is not *the only way*. It is a light from above that simply illuminates this path to salvation and helps us navigate through its delicate and difficult course. In clarifying so many details about our existence as evolutionary, spiritual beings, Spiritism reveals the wise and compassionate nature of our Creator, offering explanations about life in a uniquely direct, comprehensive, rational, and enlightening way. If it did nothing other than prove the survival of the soul, calm our fears of death, and ease the pain of our temporary separation from one another, then in just those blessings alone, Spiritism would offer a great source of consolation. This is, however, only the beginning. As we invest further in our study, we find that Spiritism's teachings and revelations help us to make sense of creation and better understand our place in it. With this newfound understanding, it is only natural that we begin to develop a deeper sense of sincere humility and a greater sense of our higher purpose.

Through Spiritism, we also acquire a greater appreciation for the moral ties that bind our past, present, and future. We thus open our hearts to new possibilities as the ideas of love and compassion take on new meaning. This process of personal growth prepares our consciousness to take flight and enables it to soar to new heights. Such freedom can only occur when our choices and actions become inspired by a more profound awareness of how we are connected to one another. To the degree that we actively engage in this process of moral and intellectual growth, we will thereby take steps toward achieving true and lasting happiness. At the same time, this world we inhabit will become a place where peace and harmony reign. From the shadows of our evolutionary

---

[85] As previously noted, see item 5 in Chapter XV of *The Gospel According to Spiritism*.

past, we will begin to see a new, regenerated humanity emerge.

According to Spiritist teachings, this future condition is certain, yet by the use of our free will, we have the power to either accelerate or delay its arrival. This is why the elevated perspective that we find in Spiritism is so important. Its enlightening and inspiring nature holds enormous potential for catalyzing this inevitable march of progress.

◊ ◊ ◊

Spiritism speaks to the heart, mind, and soul. There is something in it for every individual. With great enthusiasm, I extend to you my heartfelt invitation to explore the treasures of wisdom and inspiration that Spiritism has to offer.

Acknowledgements

I would like to express my immense gratitude to my dear husband, who introduced me to Spiritism over 15 years ago and has since been a loving, steadfast compass, guiding and supporting my learning and growth in preparation for the dissemination of Spiritism and helping me stay true to the simplicity and ideals of the Spiritist codification. In the same regard, I am deeply appreciative of the innumerable ways in which a person very special to me, Maria da Penha C. Fonseca, has helped me learn about Spiritism and the amazing power of faith. To my immediate family and friends who have accompanied my involvement with Spiritism, I am extremely grateful to you for being so whole-heartedly supportive of this path that my life has taken. And to all the Spiritists who for several years have been working hard to share the Spiritist knowledge in the English language, I thank you for your dedication and pray that such efforts will continue to develop under the guiding hand of our spiritual benefactors.

I would also like to thank, immensely, all who have contributed directly to this book. First and foremost, I am truly grateful for the collaboration from my friends in the spiritual realm whose guidance and support are invaluable. I must also express my indebtedness to all whose generous efforts went into the grammatical and stylistic reviews of the text: Daniel Fonseca, Bob Blakely, Judy Schalow and Pamela Beaudry. My sincere thanks as well to Darcy F. Neto and Christine Caldwell for their much appreciated contributions to the design and background image of the book cover.

Finally, I would like to dedicate this text to my treasured friend Altivo Carissimi Pamphiro, whose influence in this book began long before I even thought about writing a book about Spiritism. Altivo, you are so greatly missed. It brings us much joy to feel your continued presence and love alongside us, and we will forever carry in our hearts your countless examples in which we find tremendous inspiration.

About the Author

Heather Bollech-Fonseca was born in upstate, NY, where she lived until the age of 12, at which time she and her family moved to Illinois. Heather later followed her educational interests to the University of Wisconsin-Green Bay to study Environmental Policy and Planning, as well as Spanish, eventually going on to earn a degree in both areas. After graduating from college, Heather moved to Florida to work and continue her education, subsequently earning a Master's degree in Business Administration.

While living in Florida, Heather had the opportunity to study Portuguese and was introduced to Spiritism. Upon reading The Spirits' Book, Heather immediately took great interest. However, at that time, there were very few Spiritist resources available in the English language. Therefore, learning this new language gave her access to a great number of Spiritist books published in Brazil and available only in Portuguese. Since then, Heather has continued to use her knowledge of Portuguese to share Spiritist teachings and information with English speakers.

Heather is an active participant in the United States Spiritist movement. As co-founder and co-developer of the ExploreSpiritism.com website, first launched in 2003, she continues to maintain this educational resource and regularly shares examples of Spiritist thought and inspiration through its associated page on Facebook. Heather's contributions to the dissemination of Spiritism also involve her work in translating and public speaking. She collaborates as a guest presenter at Spiritist Centers in Florida and has been invited to speak by different organizations in the U.S., including The Florida Spiritist Federation, The Tri-State Spiritist Federation, and the United States Council.

www.ingramcontent.com/pod-product-compliance
Lightning Source LLC
Chambersburg PA
CBHW061650040426
42446CB00010B/1668